After 1945

JOHN HECTOR

Published by

**MELROSE
BOOKS**

An Imprint of Melrose Press Limited
St Thomas Place, Ely
Cambridgeshire
CB7 4GG, UK
www.melrosebooks.com

FIRST EDITION

Copyright © John Hector 2007

The Author asserts his moral right to
be identified as the author of this work

Cover designed by Catherine McIntyre

ISBN 978-1-906050-36-8

All rights reserved. No part of this publication may be reproduced,
stored in a retrieval system, or transmitted, in any form or by any means
electronic, mechanical, photocopying, recording or otherwise,
without the prior permission of the publishers.

This book is sold subject to the condition that it shall not,
by way of trade or otherwise, be lent, re-sold, hired out or
otherwise circulated without the publisher's prior consent
in any form of binding or cover other than that in which
it is published and without a similar condition including this
condition being imposed on the subsequent purchaser.

Printed and bound in Great Britain by:
Biddles 24 Rollesby Road, Hardwick Industrial Estate
King's Lynn. Norfolk PE30 4LS

CONTENTS

Prologue	v
Work Experience	1
Housing	8
Furniture	15
Food and 'British Restaurants'	21
Black-marketeers, Spivs and Wideboys	28
The NHS	32
Nationalisation of the Coal Mines	40
Nationalisation of the Railways	48
Steel Nationalisation	61
The Docks	71
Clean Air	76
The Festival of Britain	81
Gambling	86
Holidays	92
Cars	100
The News and BBC Radio	106
News Theatres	111
National Service	115
Pensions	120
The Coronations	123
Epilogue	127
Acknowledgements	129

Prologue

Now, at the age of eighty-nine, I have decided to record the happenings that followed the celebrations of VE and VJ Days after the Second World War.

Many of my readers, who lived in those days, would have been, like me, expecting a quick return to pre-War normality, and some compensation for the hardship and suffering, and in some cases bravery performed that was never recognised or mentioned in dispatches. Instead, rationing continued for nine years. Much of the time this was unnecessary and was due to some departments hanging on to their well paid jobs that they were initially untrained for. In six years they had learned a lot and many welcomed the newly elected Labour Government, which set about opening many new departments with different titles. This was followed by the appointment of all the new MPs introduced to Parliament. Many were uneducated in the ways of Whitehall and were forced to rely on instructions from civil servants. However, these, too, gradually lost their posts as the years progressed and the period of rationing finally came to an end.

Many factors made life so different from what we expected as our pre-War norm; the 'New Life' under the Labour Government caused some upheaval over the next five years for us all. The Government had put on their statute that a National Health Service would be formed and privatisation of the railways and mines would take place. Although these plans were decreed, very little money was advanced to set the projects in motion and it took many years

John Hector

of consultations, discussions and rearrangements before these Acts came into being. What we did not know, at that time, was that the Labour Government had secretly put aside huge sums of money to fund Harwell, an Atomic Research establishment for investigating the feasibility of developing atomic weapons. These were seen to be a necessary safeguard against the possibility of a future Atomic War, 'World War Three'. It was feared that the Russians would sweep across Europe, taking Great Britain in their wake; this was the start of 'The Cold War'.

The large sums of money spent on this defence research at Harwell took away the capital to finance new houses, hospitals and schools that were needed after the War and to shorten the prolonged period of rationing we were experiencing and which continued for a further five years. The public were unaware of this additional spending and how seriously the Government viewed the possibility of another war. We were expecting major advancements and the rebuilding of our livelihoods to be swift, and with the benefit of this hindsight I have tried to classify, in the following chapters, what life was really like for us after 1945. I hope you will enjoy reading what I have remembered and recalled in the following chapters.

John Hector

Work Experience

In December 1930, just after my fourteenth birthday, I started work at W.B. Bawn, an old, established Tank and Cylinder makers in Limehouse. My job was office boy to the Works Manager and to assist the Works Foreman. In November 1937 I started work at Fraser and Fraser at a pound a week more and I was now earning three pounds and ten shillings per week, considered to be a very good wage, plus an annual bonus every March. The Company was solely owned by Brown and Tawse, who also owned the entire building with Fraser's occupying the ground floor. The other two floors plus the penthouse and basement contained a staff of eighty people whereas Fraser's had only eighteen staff.

My job at Fraser's was to understudy a 'due for retirement' man finishing a forty-year service for the company as a Buyer and Transport Manager. I had undertaken these duties at W.B. Bawn and this made me an ideal candidate for the position. Then came the outbreak of War in September 1939. Brown and Tawse's staff dwindled to twenty and Fraser's three Managers and Director moved out to the Home Counties as did the B and T staff, leaving the building virtually empty and made worse by the call up of the remaining office staff. My position was elevated to Junior Manager throughout the 'Phoney War' period which ended in May 1940 and Dunkirk. The management ceased to visit the works but phoned in several times a day for an update on the cash taken and the orders

John Hector

both in and out. My duties increased and I was elevated to Manager at the age of twenty-three.

My dear wife, Lilian and our two girls were evacuated and I remained living in Dagenham with my mother-in-law, Frances. As I would often be required to sleep overnight at the office on fireguard duties for both companies, I had a telephone laid on especially so that I could keep in touch with Frances.

During the six years I was in charge we suffered severe bomb damage and each time we had to report to the Commissioners for War Damage and receive a claim form to record the date, time and details of the destruction sustained. The damage suffered by Fraser and Fraser, the boiler-making and heavy engineering side of the Company, was mainly to the buildings. These works were a quarter of a mile long, constructed of corrugated sheets and glass some forty feet high with travelling overhead cranes running the whole length of the structure and connecting with smaller cranes feeding both buildings and workshops along to the Wharf. Here the barges would come alongside from the River Lee adjoining the Union Canal, both of which served the east side of London.

As the War ended I had the job of settling all the claims with the Inspectors. The final amount claimed was enough for a new building and the installation of a badly needed staff and works canteen. A great reward, after enduring years of heating buckets of water on coke fires to make the tea that I had negotiated supplies of from the Brooke Bond Company (one of our very good customers). I inherited the job of overseeing all the work on the new canteen, which was to accommodate seventy people at each sitting. With the equipment, flooring, decorating, seats and 'new' Formica tops finally installed, I instructed the London Co-op to run the kitchen. The Co-op took care of the cooking, supplying tea and coffee breaks, lunches and afternoon teas, not only for Fraser's but for the parent company's workforce and eighty office staff too; some 200 people in all, throughout the six days we were working. Early canteen sittings were allotted to the labourers who, naturally, started work earlier. The later sittings were allotted to the

Steel Sales and Purchase Office and finally, after the ashtrays were emptied and the tables wiped, Tube Sales had their turn. It was important to keep the same departments together; the conversation flowed more easily!

When the canteen was fully in operation, after only a few minor setbacks, it was almost as efficient as Lyons Corner House. It was good to know that despite rationing still being in existence at that time we did not have to supply our ration books and at the end of the day at least one member of the family had been well fed. My hard work came to the attention of the Board of Directors and resulted in my elevation to a higher rank in the Brown and Tawse Head Office, and still only twenty-nine years old.

After the War was over and the celebrations ended we were short of the easy life that we had expected to follow. It was certainly a relief to know that the rockets that had wrecked so many lives in the area in and around the Capital, the last gasp thrust by the German forces, were finished. After six years of keeping Fraser and Fraser supplied with all their requirements, overseeing the running of the factory, and obtaining all the rationed materials that were needed for the three departments of the War office, I was pleased when things started, as I hoped, to get back to normal. It was far from the truth. My worries at work took a different turn; if anything it became more difficult at that time because of the public wanting supplies for various things. As there was no priority of rationing because supplies were no longer needed for the War office, it was a free for all to get supplies through for the ordinary industries to get production running in the country again.

The domestic demand on the steel industry for the supplies that they had been denied over the last six years increased dramatically. Scaling down the requirements of the armed forces, which had already been in hand for many months before the end of the War, was now taking place at great speed. So many other problems arose out of the War Damage claims, and the early settlement of these long, detailed, bulky files seemed to hang about for years after the original incident. Later additions to the first claim happened when an expense occurred a long time after and had not been noticed or could not have been evident at the time of inspection. Sometimes the damage and evidence was duplicated intentionally if the inspectors' attitude was difficult and unbending and showing little understanding of the production delay we suffered at the time.

With a change of Government, priorities altered enormously. New Ministers had to rely on the Civil Servants to show them the procedures and the necessary requirements of Industry. Naturally, this method became a situation still going today – not so much what you know but who you know, and of course how well you know them! Bribery and material benefits were rife and obtaining supplies for Fraser and Fraser became more difficult. Goods that were required fell into a wide range of new items brought about for the new Chemical trades that had now emerged. Derivatives from petrol in the form of detergents, nylon and products for the pharmaceutical industry all required stainless steel tanks for storage and manufacture, as did all avenues of food production. Plus, the UK now accepted the USA pipeline system with the introduction of API (American Petroleum Institute) standard. All of these innovations to our range of products to produce, the teaching of the workforce and the new equipment we required for manufacturing were some of the problems I had inherited.

Our pre-War orders still flowed in, such as boilers for the tea and coconut oil plantations, and the marine world still had a high demand for our patent mooring buoys from Trinity House, which controlled the navigation aids for the whole of our coastline. The Irish Lights too required similar types for their coast, as well as large orders for the Turkish Admiralty that only surfaced after so many hands had been greased; obtaining payment was equally difficult!

It must be remembered that the machinery in the factory was bought forty to fifty years before the Second World War, and plant that had come out of moth balls needed to be started up once more and the teaching of new techniques instituted. The main source of the new equipment was in the new diesel welding plants with their air compressors that were widely needed for outside jobs that had come about after six years of neglect. Stainless steel welding and the introduction of the Lloyds Register of Shipping 'Rules of Manufacture' that a number of firms insisted on for all large plant orders, were all part of the new progress of peacetime manufacture. This became a nightmare on the production lines when contracts were held up awaiting various stages of inspection; worse still if the Inspectors rejected what we had produced. Satisfying the variety of inspection teams posed a problem that we had to overcome to compete in the new commercial climate and welcome a new host of friends.

Within two years after the Blitz we had another setback in the production routine at Fraser and Fraser. I was called up at eight o'clock one evening by the night watchman as I was the nearest manager to the works. All the other managers lived forty miles away to my twenty miles. The whole of the stores were on fire – both floors of the wooden building some fifty years old, which boasted a wire screen serving counter behind which two storekeepers attended to the needs of the workforce. A lot of the stock had been written off at the stock take and very scant records of some of the old stock existed. Assessing the most serious items lost took about four days of listing and production of the job that needed the item that had been lost had to be put on hold. Of course our customers were warned of the delays and we prayed they would not cancel the contract.

In 1954 the Chairman of the group that owned us, Brown and Tawse, rewarded me by taking me out of Fraser and Fraser and as advancement for all the work I had done for them, appointed me as Buyer for the entire Brown and Tawse Steel Company. This was an honour as we had many factories and workshops all over the country and we had a wonderful reputation throughout the steel industry. You can imagine how I felt about this accolade.

The wide knowledge of stainless steel applications during manufacture that I had acquired with Fraser and Fraser stood me in great stead because the whole country was now engaged in producing many items in stainless steel and needed supplies of the necessary materials. Over the next twenty years I built up a network of four factories that supplied stainless steel in its various forms;

John Hector

'flats, rounds and angles', suitable for all trades. Within Brown and Tawse I created a department split into three sections; Black Steel, Bright Steel and Stainless Steel and educated the operators in those three departments giving them a wide, basic knowledge of the materials that we supplied to the various warehouses we operated throughout the country. I enjoyed my twenty, excellent, years of service in spite of much opposition from the other 'un-appointed' members of management who had been there and were really worthy of the advancement that I had been given. I had overtaken them in the promotion stakes as a reward by the Chairman, for my years of service at Fraser and Fraser.

Brown & Tawse Steelworks

I cut a big figure in the Metal trades and I gained a wonderful write-up in the Metal Bulletin upon my retirement in 1974, saying how sorry they were to lose one of their keenest supporters and I was known as 'Jack Hector', Chief Buyer of the Stainless Steel, Black Steel, Bright Steel and many other things at Brown and Tawse Ltd.

The years following my retirement saw a downward trend in the steel trade; bad decision-making and a depression that had started

After 1945

throughout the manufacturing world were contributors. (Further explanation of these factors is mentioned in Chapter Nine – Steel Nationalisation.) However, I enjoyed all the years I worked for the steel industry and would not have traded positions with any other job. With fascinating and varied careers both at Fraser and Fraser and Brown and Tawse, and enduring friendships forged in this country as well as Europe, including Luxembourg, Germany, Holland, Belgium, Norway and Sweden, I have such wonderful memories.

JACK

By Philip Carden

AFTER 16 YEARS as chief buyer for the steel division of Brown & Tawse Ltd and a total of 37 years' service in the B&T group, Mr Jack Hector has retired a few years ahead of his time. During his long association with the steel trade and industry he has inevitably witnessed many changes—in the art of buying steel, in the pattern and size of the Brown & Tawse group, and, among other things, in the broad view to be gained from the windows of his office at the company's headquarters at Bromley-by-Bow in the heart of London's East End.

Born in Essex, in an area that has long since been swallowed up by the ever-widening boundaries of Greater London, Jack Hector became a metalworking apprentice in Walthamstow when he was 14. Four years' apprenticeship were followed by two years of management training in the light plate and sheet-metal industry.

As an apprentice he recognised the need for, and value of, good management, and management became the target for the young shop-floor worker. To this day, he acknowledges the value of the two years' management training he received in the pre-war light engineering industry.

"Looking back to those days, I'm quite sure that two years of such opportunity was nothing like sufficient to equip me for management on the grand scale, but at least the experience gave me a good grounding, both in providing me with early insight into management and in giving me a wider knowledge of metalworking", Mr Hector told me as he turned his thoughts back to his formative years in industry.

Brown & Tawse is today firmly based on steel stockholding and processing, being one of the largest companies in the industry. Group activities, however, cover a wider field, and Jack Hector's entry into the group was gained not by way of the parent but one of its subsidiaries, Frazer & Frazer Ltd. That was in 1937 and it was 21 years later, in 1958, that Jack transferred to the fast-developing steel stockholding operation of Brown & Tawse.

Frazer & Frazer is a very old-established London business having commenced as engineers around 150 years ago. It has been owned by Brown & Tawse for many years, and until the mid-60s its main activity was boilermaking for which it enjoyed a world-wide reputation. In recent years, however, the manufacturing activities have been phased out and now the company is largely concerned with boiler repair work and other similar engineering services in which field it is active throughout the country.

Jack Hector was quite new to steel buying when wartime restrictions made the lot of the buyer both difficult and frustrating. "We were flooded out with big Government contracts early on in the war", he said. "Even so, having a wide range of steel required for their fulfilment was a tremendous headache. It was one thing to acquire a licence to buy steel and quite another actually to get the material.

"Licensing procedure slowed one down, especially in the early days of the war. The outlook brightened considerably, however, when I eventually got bulk allocations to cover a multiplicity of Government requirements."

If a leg injury put Mr Hector beyond the reach of active service in wartime, it did not put him beyond the range of enemy action. The site occupied by Brown & Tawse and Frazer & Frazer, close by Bromley-by-Bow underground station, was in an area where the Nazi bombers shed their load with terrifying effect night after night and sometimes during the hours of daylight.

Seven enemy action incidents were recorded at the premises, including a direct hit on an air-raid shelter. Fortunately, however, the bomb landed shortly after the shelter had been vacated.

Brown & Tawse is now, of course, one of the leading steel stockholders in the UK, with offices and warehouses in six main regions. In recent years there has been

STOCKHOLDING

regular and profitable expansion and the profits have risen in the last six years from £400,000 to £1·9m. Jack Hector's buying skills have clearly played their part in this expansion and his contribution both to the company and the steel industry has been considerable.

As chief buyer for B&T, Mr Hector succeeded a man who had been buying steel for the company for more than a quarter of a century. He has held the position for 16 years, and now two men are to be responsible for the company's steel purchases—Mr John H Monk in carbon and bright steel and Mr Fred Parkin in the stainless steel product range.

Fred Parkin, 20 years with Brown & Tawse, has worked alongside Jack Hector for a dozen years. John Monk joined the company five years ago. Both men have had experience in sales and purchasing.

Jack Hector is the sort of man who would make friends in whatever circle he moved. Certainly in steel he has made a host of friends. Over the years, too, he has made very many friends in London's East End. During the war years to 1965 especially did he involve himself in the community through the Rotary Club, as chairman and/or secretary of various charities, and in hospital management and other forms of welfare work.

Mr and Mrs Hector have three daughters and six grandchildren. After living at Brentwood for the past 15 years, Jack and his wife are now living at October Lodge, Bedloes Corner, Rawreth, Wickford (Essex), their new home being near Battlesbridge on the river Crouch.

To mark Jack's retirement, directors of Brown & Tawse held a presentation and dinner at the Dorchester Hotel, Park Lane, London, on October 17, when Mr S D Rae, chairman and managing director of the company, presented Mr Hector with a gift of his own choosing, thanked him for his many years of valuable service to B&T, and wished him a long and happy retirement.

Wahlen Agency for A C Cutting Machines

A C CUTTING MACHINES LTD (Kearsley Motorway Estate, Springfield Road, Kearsley, near Bolton, Lancs) has been appointed sole UK agent for the wide range of Wahlen sawing machines, designed to meet a variety of general and special-purpose cutting requirements. These machines complement the already extensive choice of sawing machines available from A C Cutting Machines.

Wahlen machines are based on a design philosophy of simplicity combined with ruggedness of construction and a smooth rigid operation. A fixed rear vice jaw coupled with a firm hydraulic drive and oversized heavy-duty gear train running in an oil bath is calculated to produce clean, accurate cuts.

Machines are available with or without a mitre cutting facility. For those requiring the mitre facility a sturdy rotary table is included giving cuts up to 45° in either direction and working in conjunction with the cutting head. Larger mitre-cutting machines can also be supplied with a powered indexing head which can be automatically adjusted.

All machine bodies are of a heavy fabricated construction sub-divided into units housing the hydraulic equipment, coolant supply, electrical control panel, and operating panel. The machine beds are heavy steel castings and range from 200mm to 300mm (8in to 12in) deep. The stock is clamped by two horizontal hydraulic vices with the option of a third vertical vice where required. The fixed rear vice facility, a unique feature of the Wahlen range, ensures extra rigidity and therefore a more accurate cut during operation. Operation is simple and the operator has an uninterrupted view during all phases of the cutting sequence.

Sizes range from 275mm (11in) dia to 1200mm (48in) dia saw blades with capacities up to and including 660mm (26in) beams and sections. Prices range from £600 for the smaller machines to £15,000 for complete cutting systems.

This article appeard in The Metal Bulletin *publication, Steel Times section on my reitrement in 1974.*

Housing

Throughout the United Kingdom considerable damage was caused by enemy action over five of the six years of war (bearing in mind that the first year was known as 'The Phoney War', during which we were left alone; the full scale bombing commenced in the September of 1940). Cities throughout the UK suffered severe damage and properties were largely irreparable. Immediately the new government came into power in 1945, they were faced with an enormous waiting list of families that required re-housing, added to which newly married service personnel looked to the councils for some accommodation. Also within a year or so, the new government was appealing for immigrant workers to enter Britain to assist in many hundreds of low paid jobs that could not be filled by the indigenous workforce.

Prior to the War, London County Council had been easing congestion by instituting council estates on the outskirts of London, which were fully populated at the beginning of 1939. The destruction to London and its residential areas was more severe than to any other city or town in the United Kingdom. Notably, the three-storey accommodation that had been built during the Victorian era for the Peabody Institution and Guinness Trust now lay ruined beyond repair. The problem was enormous; some of the smaller Councils went ahead and started building three-storey

After 1945

blocks of flats which, when fitted out with modern toilets and bathrooms, became highly desirable living accommodation for a selection of customers on the waiting lists with the greatest need. However it was only a short-term solution and only scratched the surface of the ever growing waiting list for housing; bearing in mind that the birth rate had accelerated on the return of the service men and women.

Ronan Point 15 May 1968

John Hector

The dismantling of Ronan Point

After 1945

It was not long before architects were sought to design high-rise buildings to accommodate sometimes as many as forty families. These great structures suffered a tremendous amount of vandalism and theft of the newly installed bathroom, toilet and kitchen equipment at each level and accordingly this added many weeks of delay before the flats could be inhabited and the costs were magnified from the original estimates. The Gorbals district of Glasgow had a huge problem when whole areas of demolished buildings were cleared and new sites that had been selected were not only too far away from their inhabitants' relatives and friends but meant longer distances for the population to travel to work. These newly established buildings also suffered severe damage from the attentions of disreputable tenants who were not only non-payers of rent, but trashed the accommodation when evicted. Individual tenants copied this action when they found that there was very little opportunity to take them to court. It was quickly found over the

Prefab picnic at Braintree Street, 1964

ensuing years that there were very few successful high-rise flats in the United Kingdom. The disaster at Ronan Point, a block of flats in East London, which was caused by a gas explosion, resulted in the demolition of the entire block. This safety issue became a serious problem for all cities, and in 1965 a company was set up in Manchester specialising in the demolition of all troublesome high-rise flats – a costly experiment that did not overcome the waiting list problem.

Conder Street prefabs, 1972

One way of meeting the challenge of providing accommodation during the ten years following 1945 was through the newly set up 'Temporary Housing Programme'. This took the form of prefabricated buildings produced in Sweden and Canada, which were guaranteed to last at least ten years. Some of the names that will be remembered are Arcon, Orlit, Phoenix, Spooner, Uniseco, Weir Paragon and Universal. These were a boon to families as they had indoor bathroom and toilet facilities and the sites the 'Prefabs' were built on were very conveniently placed, usually adjacent to factories, other workplaces or schools. Even today, sixty years on, many of these prefabricated buildings are still in use and are being carefully maintained by their occupants. They were centrally heated with indoor plumbing and most of them had double skins to protect them from the cold. It is a great pity that many more of these were not produced at that time, which would have alleviated the long period of distress caused by the waiting list's slow procedure. Prefabs, of course, were frowned upon originally as not being like a cherished, brick built house, but afterwards everybody acclaimed them to be first class living quarters for the purpose.

Temporary housing in Sidney Square, 1946

John Hector

Latterly, the biggest problem facing the councils that produced and introduced the prefabs, was that they were sited on areas where the city councillors were planning major road widening, clearance or the rebuilding of new properties for business premises. This of course made it necessary to, sometimes, shift the Prefabs to a site not always appreciated by the occupants who had grown used to living in some prime area of the city, which was to later become a high-class property development area.

Grateful thanks to Newham Borough Council.
Prefab photos courtesy of Chris Lloyd at Bancroft Road Library.

Furniture

Towards the end of the War the Government introduced a system of rationing furniture, which was classified as 'Utility Furniture'. This was made to a British Institute Standard and on each piece produced, the manufacturers put on a 'kite mark' logo. The standard was strictly in accordance with the rules laid down by the Institute. Certain sizes had to be adhered to for the wardrobes, tables, chairs and chests of drawers (i.e. the number of drawers) and so forth; it was a procedure that could not be altered by anyone in the furniture trade.

One had to 'apply' for the Utility Furniture and with a successful application permits were issued that contained a number of units (points) relating to the furniture required. Claims were only considered if you had suffered loss through bombing or you were getting married and were setting up home. All except nursery furniture required permits before purchase and all applications had to be made via the local Fuel Office or in writing to the Board of Trade Office at Neville House. All purchase orders were marked with a specific number of units and each piece of furniture had a different value. The Service number or Rank of the person applying was listed on the authorisation and after issue by the Assistance Board it was illegal to sell or transfer the permits. The units had a time limit of three months and any unused units were to be returned to the Assistance Board. All very controlled, but the advantage was that the furniture was free from 'Purchase Tax' and retailed at fixed prices, thus giving everyone an equal chance to restore their pre-War homes.

In the southern half of England most furniture manufacturers had suffered damage to their factories as the result of bombing or fire or, in lots of cases, the lack of raw materials was a major problem.

After the War, when some of the War damage claims were met by the various boroughs, the people who had lost their entire homes were given a small amount of money to replace their furniture and all the other items lost in the bombing of their houses. Most of these were, of course, the terraced two-up, two-down houses in the packed streets of London, whether to the North, South, East or West.

The small amount that they gave you made the choice very limited and you could only afford items of a reasonable quality to replace that which you had lost. In the East End of London not much of high value had been lost in the way of furniture and when it was replaced this then had to be used in the rented accommodation you had been lucky enough to find or if you had moved in with a family member temporarily whilst waiting for Council accommodation. Lots of the furniture was bought from second-hand market stalls or wherever it could be found.

Considered to be amongst the 'higher class' furniture suppliers were Harrods, Maples, Army and Navy stores and Heal's of Tottenham Court Road. Now that they were unable to obtain original supplies due to the shortage of material, they resorted to going to various auctions throughout the Home Counties and purchasing good quality furniture that was put into the sales by families selling up before demolition of their damaged homes. The auction sales also included pieces of furniture from churches that were being demolished, the cleared sites making way for new housing estates.

These large retailers would bring back to their shops whatever they could buy in the way of good quality furniture. These items

After 1945

then went for polishing, repairing and re-upholstering in some fine cloth, sometimes tapestry or perhaps hide or Rexene.

Sometimes it was found that one furniture supplier would have bought six chairs and a different firm would have purchased the matching table for the suite and for a customer wishing to purchase the set it was necessary to shop around to see if you could match the chairs from one shop to the table from another to give you the suite that you desired.

The price for second-hand furniture was high and I had an experience of this myself when we wanted some furniture for our boardroom. I knew good purchases could be made by cash deals with some first-class furniture manufacturers operating in Hackney. My visit to their works in Hackney with promise of prompt cash payment produced the desired result. It came by night covered in blankets, in the back of a car, brought into the boardroom and left until the following night when a further two chairs would come. It was done this way to get them out of the view of anyone coming in to look. They would not see a whole suite of chairs so it was better that they brought them in two at a time and duly the eight chairs arrived. The table came down in pieces and was assembled in the boardroom, all by craftsmen, who did not work under our supervision. When the cash exchanged hands we then received an invoice signing for eight chairs, polished and re upholstered, and the table, French polished, explaining all what they were supposed to have done for £100 and not £900 which was given as a cash payment! I found that there was always a way of obtaining just what was needed!

As the manufacturers started to accumulate supplies of timber, several companies started producing reasonably good-looking furniture, which was better than the Utility kind. Some very fine bedroom suites were made by the Austin Suite Company, another by 'Limelight' Furniture, also for the bedroom. This furniture was made of lime wood and sprayed a lime colour over an oak finish, which made it very attractive and brought considerable success to the manufacturers. The Austin Suite Company painted their

John Hector

furniture white in colour, which gave a very nice finish to the brass handles and fittings. Soon, shipments of mahogany started to arrive from the Far East and of course walnut veneers were then being produced very rapidly by the Times Furnishing Company, which was producing large quantities of 'G Plan' furniture. Most of it was in walnut veneer and the range of furniture was much wider, including teak wood dining room suites of various shapes. Some of the suites had tall units with built-in cocktail cabinets with glass and tumbler racks or china cabinets with mirrors inserted at the back of the cabinet that magnified the contents. It is a credit to the makers of 'G Plan' that their designs of the 1960s are much sought-after items of furniture today.

The following pictures are from a Wartime catalogue showing Utility Furniture.

After 1945

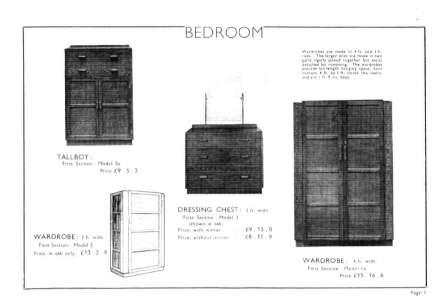

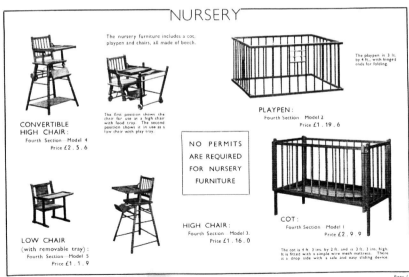

John Hector

Food and 'British Restaurants'

Following the severe bombing of London in September 1940, the then London County Council instructed various borough councils to set up, with immediate effect, 'Meal Services' for all workers, so they were supplied with a midday meal to enable vital production to keep running.

This was imperative, as many areas suffered gas, electric and water services that had been severely disrupted and workers were unable to eat at home.

There followed the setting up of approximately 200 eating places in public halls and churches. These 'Londoners' Meals Centres' as they were initially known, were hastily set up with tables and chairs to seat between fifty and a hundred people at one time. The kitchen staff were able to provide food, off the ration, freshly cooked, for an average cost of one shilling and nine pence per meal.

The diners were requested to depart immediately after they had consumed their food to enable others waiting to enter the building. The queues lengthened each day as the word spread that hot meals were available off the ration.

Not only were the workers on production lines the beneficiaries, elderly folk who waited till the midday workers had departed found it easier to enjoy a substantial meal in the centres than rely on their meagre rations, very often with extra helpings if the meals were coming to a conclusion. After a trial period the rest of the country benefited from the 'Centres'.

Their dual purpose of being equipped to deal with emergencies was a great advantage. As the War continued, 2000 such establishments were installed around the country and covered most of the big city areas. During this time they became known as 'British Restaurants' or 'Civic Restaurants' and this name continued well into the early 1950s when the restaurants gradually began to phase out when food rationing at the end of 1945 started to ease off.

Rationing, however, did not cease immediately and it took nearly nine years for this to be fully accomplished. The price of the meals into the 1950s began to increase but it was stipulated that no meal should exceed five shillings (twenty-five pence today), bearing in mind that the ration of food was generally as follows:

Four oz bacon or ham
Three pints milk
Two oz butter
Two oz margarine
Two oz fat or lard
Two oz loose tea
One egg per week
Two oz jam
Three oz sugar
One oz cheese
Three oz sweets

At the end of the War these restaurants became much more of a social meeting place and many families arranged to meet their relations when travelling from town to town. With a cup of tea and a hot meal at very reasonable prices, it was a good venue at which to discuss family matters. Also, they became good places to pick up information about black market goods or items that had been rare, unobtainable, or necessitated a long wait for delivery.

After 1945

One of Britain's best known cooking experts, Marguerite Patten, was employed during the War by the Ministry of Food and regularly assisted the well known Radio Doctor in giving out recipes to the public on the wireless as to how to become healthy and above all, economical with the use of the food available. She would give advice on what would make a healthy meal, and what would be easy on the cooking fuel when rationing was severe after bombing. Healthy stews with potatoes and carrots could be made heartier with the introduction of a few handfuls of pearl barley stirred in the stew pot to give more substance. These recipes became well known, and in some families, reintroduced with some vegetable or gravy mix that had become available through a member of the family as it 'fell off the lorry' as he or she was 'passing by'!

Bovril, Marmite and Bisto were all in demand and 'Edward's desiccated Soup Powder' became a regular special broth in Grandma's kitchen where the homely smell flowed out of the kitchen window and filled the street with an appetising aroma.

Marguerite, now in her nineties, regularly speaks to the public on 'Soundaround', an audio tape magazine where she gives out a new recipe each month to listeners throughout the world. Thousands of her CDs and tapes are produced and dispatched annually at very little cost. This dear lady has been assisting the producers of the tape since its foundation over twenty-five years ago. Recently, I had the pleasure of talking to her over the telephone at her residence in Brighton, Sussex and we had long discussions about her recent television appearances. These started when TV was in its infancy and she attended the first show at Alexandra Palace, North London, before the War, and again when it was introduced as BBC Television.

With the demise of 'British Restaurants', new cafes and coffee bars started to appear in our towns. 'The Golden Egg' and 'Wimpy Bars' were the forerunners of MacDonald's, Kentucky Fried Chicken, Pizza Hut and Chinese take-away restaurants. Indian restaurants started to appear in our towns and high streets and the public's tastes changed over the years following the end of the War.

John Hector

With the influx of immigrants and asylum seekers, many other restaurants are coming into the country and establishing their own particular food sources, making our diet and eating habits varied and establishing links to make others feel at home in our country.

Grateful thanks to the Imperial War Museum for the following photographs and captions.

NEG: D4856. Run by Women's Voluntary Service Members - This British restaurant provides a midday meal of meat or fish, two veg and a sweet at low cost - saves fuel and wastage.

*NEG: D10678
Preparation of the meal*

After 1945

NEG: D10673
Off duty sailors enjoying a midday meal at the British restaurant Woolmore Street. Run by Women's Voluntary Service

NEG: D10681
First sitting at the Woolmore Street restaurant.

25

John Hector

We are grateful to Marguerite Patten for allowing the use of the photographs of two of her cookery books. Also for her continuing contribution to the Soundaround Tapes for the visually impaired.

After 1945

Black-marketeers, Spivs and Wideboys

Post-War Highwaymen *by George T. Stovell*

Having suffered during the War with the rationing of all commodities that were needed for family life such as food, clothing and household essentials, there was, naturally, a ready market for almost any item due to scarcity. Towards the end of the six years, even the black-marketeers found it very difficult to get supplies of any description, having exhausted the sources of most useful commodities.

After 1945

In 1946 one avenue of supply for them was via so-called 'extra' case food that was not required by the armed services in the barracks and rest rooms. Cases of surplus foodstuffs would find their way from the stores to the open market for the 'traders' to buy and of course for them to sell on at a much higher price. This was a boom period for the black-marketeers who then put the word around of what was on offer. 'Spivs' were the people who would deal in the odd case or two of anything that was on offer. Whereas Black-marketeers could locate quantities, Spivs would find items under the blanket term of 'Fell off the back of a lorry' or they would 'locate' specific items for a willing client. A particular scam was 'items that were water damaged', which meant that the labels had been washed off the products they had for sale. Most were washed off deliberately to eradicate any evidence of the contents.

Of course, this made purchasing one of these label-less cans a hazardous experience. A lot of the tinned food appeared in the market place with a story that it could be a tender pineapple, peaches, potatoes or carrots. Some went so far as to label the goods incorrectly, promising all kinds of things inside. Sometimes food for animals, which was destined to supply the zoo and had been paid for by the Government, ended up on sale via Spivs. It truly was like a game of roulette buying anything from these people but it was the same throughout the country; if you bought a tin that you liked the look of but it had no label, it was your mistake!

This scam of surplus to requirements did not last long, naturally, because the food eventually disappeared from the overspill of the allocation to the Services, but what did become more obvious was that there was a lot more money about with the extra wages and money that was being brought home by the servicemen from their savings. Any commodity was then found to be elevated to a higher price, knowing that the public would pay and have the extra to get it. It happened, too, in the clothing and household textile market. Families found that they needed shoes for children who had grown or for a man or woman where their shoes had become irreparable;

John Hector

the same with sheets, pillowcases, towels and everything else you needed to survive. Most of them had been patched, sewn, repaired and cut down to lose the worn parts as the need for economy was paramount; so, understandably, there was still a big demand on the spivs or marketeers that were operating after the celebrations had finished.

The 'Wideboys' operated on different terms. They also liked to turn goods into money but theirs was more of a long-term investment. They would speculate that a large quantity of surplus items would, one day, be worth money. Thus they would 'buy', very cheaply, obsolete goods from stores and yards and sell them at a much later date perhaps, even, for a different purpose. An example would be gas mask containers – no longer needed for carrying masks at the end of the War, the carriers became useful, durable, shopping bags (also perfect for carrying unlabelled tins!). Large quantities of equipment, goods and machinery were purchased this way by the Wideboys holding 'wide' ranges of goods that had fallen off the backs of lorries. That meant, too, that the goods destined for an area would suddenly disappear from the lorry or the railway truck that was delivering them. Then you would find that there would be a commodity or a product that would be available in more quantities than usual in the area where the 'accident' had happened. This, of course, was robbery and opened the door wide for large-scale pilfering and theft. When the items contained in the deliveries were known to be good sellers, planned raids were organised instead of random theft. This, of course, led to a wide range of crime and lawbreaking that the police had to deal with.

From my experience I found that most of the East London population during the War would keep away from buying goods on the black market as they felt it was taking from the country's requirements, but as time wore on and neighbours could see that Mrs Jones had no shoes for the children or a new coat was needed for a son or daughter, even the most principled of the public and occasionally the most religious-minded strayed from the flock. Probably the confessionals at Mass included these people for whom repentance for the error of their ways was needed. We had to endure nine years of this period of want as it was a very slow process to dismantle the rationing of commodities one at a time; much to the annoyance of the population of East London. The practice became to take whatever you could get, pay for it and either sell it on, sometimes at a higher price, or keep the surplus for a later date. Whatever commodity was now being harboured the money was then an investment as far as they were concerned; they had stock and they could realise it if things got tight. The fact it might have been stolen property in most cases was very difficult for the police to prove and also they were very unwilling to apprehend people who had suffered so much and had received so little reward for all their hardship.

There were large numbers of the public who were content to save a few shillings in Post Office savings accounts and wait for times when things were back to normal and there would be no under-the-counter dealings or black market.

Unfortunately, by paying higher prices to the dealers the seed was sown for the future route the retail marketplace was to take over the next twenty years. Greed had seeded into the population with the attitude of having things immediately without saving for them and by an increase in the number of 'hire purchase' accounts, which, in the long run, gave traders the headache of recovering accounts that could never be paid, resulting in cases of bankruptcy.

The NHS

For my readers it is necessary to indicate what the health pattern was for the people in East London mainly after the First World War. Councils of each borough found it necessary to install more doctors in each county to assist in treating many of the injured service people that came back from five years of war in Europe. Many doctors that came into the area were given an allowance for how many patients were attributed to them and in some cases two doctors shared the same premises, which helped each of the doctors have a day off in between each surgery so that they could attend to patients who were housebound or bedridden and, of course, take a day off occasionally for their own pleasure.

The doctors' waiting rooms were fairly standard in each borough and could only take a set number of people and, very often, some would stand outside in the street awaiting their turn. It was found that only a certain amount of time would be required for the treatment of each patient.

The doctors were called panel doctors and we who joined were called panel patients. If you were ill, it was necessary to attend the doctor and ask for a certificate to certify that you were unable to work as you would need this evidence to keep your job open. A charge of six pence was made for the certificate proving that you were unsuitable for work and likewise in a week or so when you were feeling better you went back again, taking your turn in the waiting room, and you would be charged a further six pence to say that you were now fit enough to work. If it was found you needed to be sent to a hospital for treatment, two doctors would have to sign a form for your entry into a hospital, thus securing a second opinion before unloading the welfare of the patient on to a hospital for whatever purpose.

It became necessary for most families to obtain extra insurance from an association called the Hospital Savings Association, the HSA. This was a savings book into which each family would pay sixpence pence per week for the entire family of man and wife and his children to allow admission into hospital, without any charge, or to obtain dental treatment, or for eyesight or hearing checks to be made. If it was necessary to obtain treatment or an inspection, a green form had to be obtained from the secretary of the HSA. Armed with this you could go to any of the prescribed people and there would be no payment to be made. This was a boon for most families because with the increase in the population and overcrowding, insurance meant a better opportunity for your family to get attended to.

London County Council helped the population of the borough of Poplar and most notably the children to keep as healthy as possible, considering this to be an imperative given the density of the housing. London County Council installed in Poplar fourteen schools for children from the ages of five to fourteen, each school taking between 300 and 400 pupils. It introduced measures to follow and check the health of the children at regular intervals; this was, in fact, an intermediate measure between the local panel doctors and the hospital authorities. Nurses were assigned to check hands, ears and heads for any visible signs of possible infections such as Measles or Scarlet Fever, as any disease, unchecked, would spread through a school rapidly.

The headmaster of the school or headmistress, was also very aware of possible infections and would immediately notify the nurse to come back to inspect a suspect child and arrange for a further medical check. An infected child would be isolated and sent to an isolation hospital, if necessary, in a yellow ambulance, which denoted that there was infection aboard. The people in close contact with the child or the relatives were also asked to keep clear of the area for some time. A yellow envelope would be sent to a home depicting that there was an infection and the person or child would have to be carted away to an isolated hospital to avoid the spread of the disease. This was an essential part of the LCC's action and was applied to the population not only of Poplar but throughout the capital as a method of assisting the residents. London County Council, from County Hall, managed health issues together with the parks and all the other amenities to provide comfort for the population of London.

We are grateful to the London Hospital Archives and Museum for the following photograph:

London Hospital 1950s

After 1945

We are grateful to the www.eastlondonpostcard.co.uk for the following images of other London Hospitals.

Poplar Hospital

St. Andrew's Hospital

John Hector

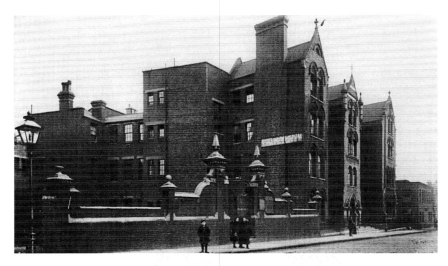

East London Hospital for Children, Shadwell

City of London Hospital

After 1945

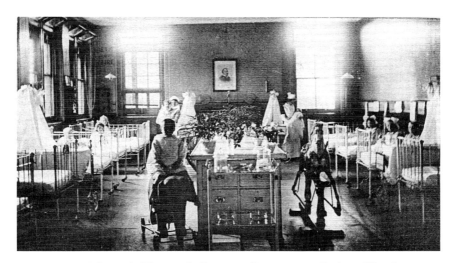

Her Majety's Hospital, Stepney Causeway - Babies Ward.

Aneurin Bevan's 'National Health Service', which was introduced by the 1948 Parliament was, potentially, a tremendous benefit to the whole of the country, although it took nearly twenty years before it could get properly established. This was because the three or four governments coming into power in the intervening years were either giving good support or not much support to the various needs of the new Health Service. When one looks back to see what we had come from in terms of health care, whatever we received from the new National Health Service was a great improvement to the whole of the population of the United Kingdom.

For the last sixty years the nation has enjoyed free medical health care and during those sixty years we have advanced by forging good relationships with the health authorities from the treatments offered to the resolving of causes of complaint. It must be remembered that in this period, too, great progress has been made across the sphere of medical research into diseases of all the major organs of the body and pioneering surgery such as heart and liver transplants have been carried out. Hip and knee replacements are now common operations and a major breakthrough in the late 1970s was the offer of fertility treatment; giving hope of the gift of life to present day couples where sixty years ago, there was none. Once a cause of blindness, cataracts can now be removed in a short operation and the patient is ready to resume their normal life the next day.

The discovery of DNA patterns crosses the realms of purely medical concern into that of criminal forensic investigation; the successful conviction of murderers with indisputable evidence and the identification of remains whether for solving crimes or researching our ancestors has all been made easier by this remarkable discovery.

The benefits we have enjoyed over the last sixty years of all these medical advancements has been tremendous but it has to go on record that in the last ten years of my life we have had a Government in power that has introduced various forms of management into the NHS system. We now have Primary Care Trusts (PCTs) to whom local surgeries and hospitals are answerable within their particular regions. We are now experiencing American health centres being set up and the fielding out of NHS delivery systems to German companies, a move that proved so unpopular as to invoke the first ever strike within the NHS. The rise in this country's population over the last sixty years, due, in equal parts, to increasing longevity, a high birth rate and immigration has seen an ever increasing burden placed on the NHS to provide the best possible health care.

The breadth of knowledge needed to treat every case that presents itself at hospitals and surgeries has been insurmountable; thus we saw the advent of the distribution of antibiotics as a possible cure for everything. Now, it has been established that they are not a cure-all and are dispensed less frequently. Similarly the standard of cleanliness within our hospitals is not nearly as good as it was sixty years ago, as we have witnessed with potentially fatal infections such as MRSA that seem to gain a hold over the weak and infirm in a remarkably short space of time. There appears to be too many managerial decisions and lengthy reports on how the health service should be run and not enough action in putting the ideas into practice.

After 1945

It seems such a great pity that the once organised and respected National Health Service should now find itself floundering through lack of funds, the right management skills and an inability to treat people as quickly as they deserve.

Nationalisation of the Coal Mines

When the Labour Government came into power under the leadership of Atlee at the end of the Second World War, its members contained a number of left wing socialists; many of them so far left that they were almost communists and from this left-wing section many called for the immediate Nationalisation of the railways, hospitals, steelworks and, their chief target, the coalmines.

Little did they know, however, that starting in December 1946 through to March 1947 the United Kingdom was to be hit by the severest winter on record. This involved many, many factories and mills throughout the Midlands and the North completely closing down for several months due to an inability to obtain coal, thus shutting off the coal-fired electricity-generating power stations. This in turn, limited the use of electricity, in some cases to just five hours per day throughout the UK.

This hiccup slowed the progress of Nationalisation as much had to be investigated in the state of the mines at the time of the takeover. This suited the mine owners very well indeed because with the problem of the recession in the 1930s and up to the time of the outbreak of War there was a lot of work to be done on the mines by way of modernisation and repair. During the War, of course, maintenance could not be done to any great extent and from the fourteen years of neglect already suffered many were in a state of disrepair.

After 1945

For a century or more the mine owners had kept the working miners at arm's length and caused them unnecessary suffering with the meagre wages they paid them so, by getting the nation's coal mines working, this was to be a radical change for the future of the industry.

As a young man I welcomed the decision to Nationalise the mines. In 1926, then nine years old, I witnessed the troop movement into the East End of London where the whole district supported the miners and caused the General Strike which, unfortunately, the miners lost. This was due to their trade union, then known as the TUC, giving way to Prime Minister Baldwin who backed the Coal Owners who demanded that the miners work longer hours, and that their already low pay be further reduced.

The brutal conditions that the owners inflicted on the miners caused, in some cases, a complete 'lock out' and many miners' families were forced to starve.

The whole of East London was, at that time, infuriated by the action of the Baldwin Government and I witnessed marching miners from the North of England come to sing in our streets to earn a few coppers to send back to their loved ones. This is well remembered by me as, poor as we were, my Mother gave me two pennies to put into the miner's cap which was the same sum as I earned as pocket money for being good and running errands. Five years later, at the age of thirteen and a half, I was fortunate enough to go on a school holiday for fourteen days into Derbyshire and was able to go down the Clay Cross Coalmine. The experience of the working conditions of those miners has never left me, even today.

The group of us ten senior boys first went to be registered at the lamp store where we were handed a Davy Lamp, well known for many years as a symbol for miners throughout the UK. Our names and numbers were recorded at the Lamp Store and we were then shepherded into the large pit cage and assembled around two large coal trucks standing on railway lines. We were then told to breathe in deeply and hold our breath while the cage plummeted down at an immense speed. We could feel the cold air rushing round our heads, hands and faces and our steel caps were held on to, tightly, as the cage reached the bottom and landed on several springs, jumped up a few feet, finally coming to a stop, coating all of us in the cage with a shower of water and condensed air that we had collected on the downward journey. We stepped out of the cage into a large, whitewashed area, which was the main command post for a series of tunnels that sprouted out in all directions. The main side of this area contained three small pit ponies tethered, singly, to food mangers slightly above their heads. Above this was a range of yellow canaries in cages. We were told that these were investigated every hour or so to check for any sign of noxious gases that may have escaped from the many workings. The canaries would die but give ample warning to all the miners to assemble at points ready for evacuation as quickly as possible. We were told that the ponies would not have to work, as they were the remnants from a fleet of many dozens who had now all been put out to pasture to enjoy a long and happy retirement. They had only been released a few at a time to acclimatise themselves to natural light after so many years working far below the earth's surface.

We ten boys followed the conducted tour through a long, long tunnel, which, I believe, took us half a mile through the pit head where we had started from at the cage. At the end of the tunnel we branched off to another 300-yard journey down the glimmering tunnel to a work face where we saw four men wielding axes and breaking into coal veins, piece by piece. They stood aside whilst the other team shovelled the broken lumps into the line of steel wagons of which six were partially filled. When this was completed the wagons would be removed by a small power driven truck to the pit loading area. Another large cage would be ready to take up a dozen or two wagons at a time, ready to be tipped on a conveyor belt and subsequently shot into railway wagons.

We watched the men, stripped down to shirt sleeves, hacking at the coal face, some of them lying flat on sack-lined wooden platforms that rolled along the ground as they worked. We boys were invited, individually, to swing the axe to see what penetration we could muster from our puny frames. From our poor endeavours we were invited to put a piece of the coal in our pockets to prove that we had actually mined the coal ourselves. Our lips were sealed by an indication from the dirty-faced miners to conceal the theft from the coal owner's deputy who would greet us on leaving the pit. The memory is still with me today, seventy-five years later and I have never ceased to convey my admiration for the miners throughout the world who dig the earth's crust for a living and in many cases a much-shortened life.

When Nationalisation did come about, long gone were the hundreds of coal merchants dotted around each city, and of course London had many hundreds. The method of distribution of coal was quite a simple matter. The truckload from a railway was sent down to a coal depot's sliding in a local company. From here the coal merchant had huge stocks of coal, which would be deposited in its various grades. Different coal mines would send down varying qualities such as Derby Brights, Yorkshire fine and numerous names given to the various qualities of coal, which gave you greater power and was easier to use and in most cases reduced waste if you were using coal continually for heating apparatus and various appliances such as coal fired furnaces, incinerators, retorts or boilers and so forth. Of course each quality of coal would be advertised by the coal merchants on their lorries or in those earlier days on the horses and carts, and traded by the coalman around the streets for the public to buy. Nearly every city had a demand for coal, for retort houses in the gasworks from which they would extract gas from the coal delivered and pump the rest in to gasometers or gas holders as they were also known. Some of these vast storage tanks can still be seen today, empty of gas, as an historic relic.

After the extraction of the minerals and the gas itself, the residue was put on sale at the gasworks in each city for the general public to purchase and help to maintain their heating and domestic appliances for cooking etc. This was sold at a cheaper rate than the coal that the coalman delivered so there was a demand for the extracted coal or 'coke' and the public were happy to come and collect so none was delivered on the basis that the coalman offered. The chore of collecting the sacks of coal this way was usually given to young boys and girls on a Saturday morning. After queuing they would take a sack, and the steaming coal that had been saturated with water in the extraction process would be collected in small loads. The heavy 'coke' would then dry out and weigh less than when first collected.

Throughout the UK the mines were distributed in almost every county. Many of them were in Wales, and Scotland, too, had an enormous amount of coal. Mines in the North of England were dotted around Nottinghamshire, Derbyshire, Yorkshire and Lancashire. In Southern England we had mines in Kent and they all produced various grades of coal, which was essential, but technology was advancing. With the Nuclear Bomb that had been dropped in Japan, the next inroad into wider technology had begun. When the Labour Party started getting its feet under the table they decided that they would shut down all the coal-fuelled power stations and replace them with Nuclear energy. Nuclear power stations would not require enormous amounts of coal fuel to operate them and give people the electricity they required. The population in those days was promised electricity at a very low cost when the nuclear power stations were installed and of course the atmosphere would be clearer. In later years, the potential dangers from nuclear fallout were realised when appliances failed at the stations such as in the accident at Chernobyl, Russia.

The loss of the demand for coal from the power stations was a great market loss for the pits and of course there was no market for the Nationalised industry; although the coalmine owners were selling off their pits it was to a falling market and consequently that meant a number of closures took place. This caused great unemployment for the miners and for the coal mining villages and towns that depended entirely on the miners' money.

Although the pit closures took place over a number of years the effects of the closures and the loss of coal to the domestic market was satisfactory only to the pit owners, who not only owned the pits but the surrounding land above them. This led to opencast mining in the large areas of pastureland above the pits. Six feet below the surface of the soil would find a good stratum of coal that could be economically used for domestic purposes; although not quite as good or powerful as the deep cast coal, it satisfied low-cost burning. Thousands of tons of coal were taken in this manner and although it was low grade, it brought in a very nice profit for the owners. These opencast mines were easily filled in and then the land reclaimed as pastureland.

With the steady progress of the mine closures came a considerable amount of trouble in the early 1970s. The leader of a mining district, Arthur Scargill, caused a tremendous amount of disruption by setting up a different union to the miners' union that had been running for many years and at one stage the Conservative Government, which took over later, had to close down the electricity supply for up to three days a week, and upset industry by turning off power throughout the United Kingdom; the dispute was not resolved for many years. It is ironic that now in 2007 the country is being instructed to rebuild Nuclear power stations which were taken down and decommissioned over a number of years when it was found that energy could be obtained from various parts of Europe and of course, a free gas supply from the North Sea Gas terminals and North Sea Oil. There was no necessity to have the nuclear power stations that had been started up by Tony Benn in earlier years.

So it comes back in full circle that today, when trying to keep the atmosphere clean they are now thinking of having nuclear-fuelled power stations once more and off-shore wind farms to supply energy for industrial and domestic use.

John Hector

Many thanks to Deal Library for supplying photographs of Betteshanger Colliery in Kent which was one of the earliest closures in the forty-year period of the total collapse of the Coal Owners' monopoly of the industry.

At the surface

After 1945

Betteshanger Colliery near Deal, Kent

At the face

Nationalisation of the Railways

When the Labour Government decided to nationalise the main four railways, that is the LNER, LMS, GW and the Southern Railway, they were separate from the Underground system and controlled by the London Passenger Transport Board, which had been set up by London County Council. Each of the four main railway stations was the head office for the entire railway system that ran throughout the United Kingdom. Each of the buildings contained hundreds of specialised workers who had given years of service and were picked to do the specific job that they were trained for in their particular field of operation.

There was, naturally, a passenger section that fixed the passenger rates and the distances of travel were carefully calculated. There was the haulage section, which managed the heavy truckloads of commodities that had to be shifted from one end of the country to the other. All these operations were carried out daily and in most cases, continued throughout the night as well to ensure that the railways would work perfectly.

Variations were at the Midland and the North Eastern Railways where there was a great deal of extra work to be done to allow each train belonging to the different sections to be able to pass over the network of rail lines that had been laid out by the pioneers over 140 years earlier.

After 1945

Copyright JW Armstrong Trust

The network also contained a system of radio contact, which was, then, by telephone, through overhead cables or signals. This was a very big operation, as the network of signal boxes along the lines of every yard, laid down by the railways, had to contact each other to signal the safe crossing of the train or goods traffic that was passing through at their point. It was a very complex system involving hundreds of levers to shift the railway tracks from one side of the rail link to the other to allow the fast express trains to go through at perhaps forty, fifty or sixty miles an hour, and on the other side allow for slow moving haulage traffic to safely pass the danger point where the express trains would be following. The system had to be worked very carefully.

Within the Head Offices were departments that dealt with the staff, their wages and the continuous contact with the stationmasters all over England, Scotland and Wales. In all there must have been several thousand workers controlled by each of the railway Head Offices, all to be taken over by the new Labour Government under the heading of 'Nationalisation'. There were workshops along the lines also under the control of the Head Offices. There was one in Darlington, another in Droitwich, and on the southern side

John Hector

in Swindon and Southampton and various areas throughout the country. These employed gangs of men to continuously check the railway lines for safety to make sure there was no damage to the line itself, and that the cleats holding the rails were tight and in place. The cleats were fastened by hexagon headed bolts, which were tightened by a long handled spanner, to make sure they were not loose, causing the rail to be disjointed at any point. There were also a lot of workers whose job it was to go along continually with a hammer checking the cast iron rails and wheels to make sure there were no cracks or flaws on the haulage contractor's various trucks that would come through; open trucks, covered trucks and mail wagons and so forth. If the 'tap' did not sound right or 'ring true', there may be a crack in which case the truck would be pulled off the line and shunted through to a siding for the workshop to change the wheel. Also, on all the trains there were brake blocks made out of cast iron, which had to be changed regularly to ensure they would operate under any conditions when the brakes were applied from the central source.

Courtesy HM Postmaster General

After 1945

These gangs worked continuously every few hundred yards of the hundreds of miles of line laid down by the railways. There were locomotive depots laid on along the line to make sure that the trains could be checked, oiled, greased and so forth at either point on the journey it was taking. Boilers had to be thoroughly checked and the fireboxes cleaned, which was a job usually done overnight when the trains were stationary. Along these lines, too, in earlier days there were water tanks that would fill the boiler tanks to ensure there was good steam available with no leaks. This was superseded later on by the diesel locomotives that had begun to come into operation at the outbreak of war but were left idling, waiting further development. After the six-year War period they were reinstated in 1945/6 with Nationalisation beginning in 1948.

Steam

The safety of the railway traffic and passengers was of paramount importance and the safety checks given to them throughout the industry was very stringent and constantly double checked. There were very few failures when we come to think of the millions of people transported from rural areas into the cities and from city to city on a daily basis. 'A regular timetable was set up, planning the trains' routes as accurately as possible, and, amazingly, there was little variation.'

Occasionally a train would be derailed somewhere, and cause a minor delay, but in accordance with safety regulations cranes were dotted all over the country at various points to ensure a quick reconstruction of the site if there was damage to be repaired. It had to be ensured that it all worked perfectly before service was resumed to transport the hundreds of tons of commodities, wood, steel, and cement etc, drafted from the manufacturing sources wherever they were throughout England, Scotland or Wales, to the areas of use where they were going to be manufactured. Of course the contracts were jealously fought for; each area had to give a good price for operating at various tonnages and in quantities that would be suitable to be put on the trucks to be delivered safely and without delay.

Diesel

I used the rail network a tremendous amount, with goods coming from Scotland, South Wales and of course the North East coast along the Teesside. We would negotiate the price for the tonnage to be delivered in fifty or hundred ton lots, whatever they were, and the Rail Company would decide how many wagons were needed. Amongst the products I had to transport were very long steel bars and these would be chained or fastened on with various security arrangements so that nothing moved in transit. We also took the opportunity of using what we called FAS, which was 'Free along side'; if we ordered some steel from Scotland or Wales, we could negotiate a price for it to be delivered into a railway depot nearest to our works, whichever they chose. London North Eastern Railway would, very often, chip a few shillings per ton off the London Midland offer and the Welsh may have had a different rate entirely. In those days, if we paid half a crown, which was two shillings and sixpence (twelve pence), we could get the steel delivered on the following day.

The Rail Company would choose a depot where there was a canal or river loading, where the goods we ordered would be placed into a barge from the railway siding then steamed up right alongside our wharf where we would then have a crane to lift the steel out and put it into our warehouse, ready for use. Hence this was a very economical way for us to buy, as we were not held up by the long loads coming through, by road, around the back streets of East London.

Orders could be delivered by water straight to our wharf, via two rivers or two waterways; one was the River Lee that transported water from the Thames into the New Lee that flowed out of Hertfordshire, and the other was a canal called the Prince Regent Canal. This waterway went right the way around London; through north, east and to the west of London before returning. The canal in the earlier days was used for transportation by horse-drawn barges to deliver goods, fresh vegetables etc. from one site to another by water. We, now, used those sites to bring goods from the steelworks and factories to alongside our wharf; some sidings in the railways were better served by canal than they were by the river and it made for a simpler operation.

Newbiggin Railway Station

Of all the administration that happened in these buildings, aside from moving these tremendous amounts of tonnage around the country, it was the passenger transport that had to be worked out very carefully for pricing. A lot of people were coming in from the rural areas because, in their wisdom, the railway pioneers had set up various stations in very distant areas of the UK which let the local populations have the opportunity of going into the towns not only for a visit, but also for work. A daily delivery of labour resources getting into the towns and villages, which they could not do easily by any other method, as there was no motorcar transport in those days for the majority of people, was a wonderful opportunity. It was of paramount importance for them to be able to visit the city to get into work fairly quickly and also have a reliable train service that would get them early in the morning to the office and home again in the evening. To serve the public well, the stations had to be maintained to a high standard. The station masters at each of these rural stations would vie with one another as to who had the best station. The approaches would be set with flowers, pots and plants and the little waiting rooms on the station platforms usually had a well stoked fire to keep the passengers warm while they were waiting for the trains to come in, if there had been a delay or if there was snow or icy weather.

There were many of these little stations up and down the lines; some were very tiny and just served by a single track or Halt but they provided a vital link to the public, especially the elderly.

The services that the main line railways offered the general public were enormous. I used them regularly to go to Glasgow and sometimes Birmingham. Glasgow was a very quick run for me because I would leave work at seven o'clock at night in East London, go to King's Cross Station, have a meal in that area and book my all night, first class, sleeping compartment for about a pound or thirty shillings in those days, and present my ticket at nine o'clock, ready to go aboard because departure would be at half past nine. Being there half an hour early, I would be waited on by a Pullman operator with peaked cap and salute saying, "your reservation is here Sir".

A little label stuck on the window would state "reserved for John Hector". And he would later come in and say, "would you like a drink tonight before you go to sleep Sir? Cocoa, Ovaltine, tea or coffee?" And he would inform you of any disturbances that may disrupt your sleep! Perhaps there would be a stop at Crewe for half an hour's service and the station would be open should you want anything there in particular – "give a tinkle on this bell and tell me what you want". At a midnight shopping trip at Crewe station, passengers would alight to have a walk round, before going on to Glasgow!

When we arrived at Glasgow, the steward would knock on the door at about seven o'clock. "Would you like a cup of tea Sir? We are in the station, there is no need for you to rush; breakfast will be served in the Pullman car from eight o'clock to half-past nine."

I would get up leisurely, have a wash and shave, get dressed and go to the Pullman, have breakfast, sort the bill out and go on to

John Hector

do my day's work in Glasgow. Then, possibly, go on to some of the outlying areas in Glasgow to visit steelworks. This was, for me, an enjoyable experience of long distance rail travel.

Sidings at Patchey Bridge

In addition to the passenger service, there was also a service running for the Royal Mail. This was a service instituted jointly with Royal Mail and the Railways and was the forerunner of us being able to get our letters posted at night, sorted on board the train and delivered the following morning. Sometimes, we had an exceptionally good service by having twice-daily deliveries. This meant that some firms could receive additional orders in the second post; banks took the opportunity of using this service to send large amounts of cash in registered envelopes to post to various banks in their area and to Scotland. The mail bags would be set near the doors and then thrown out into a wide catch net which would be set up by the main railway stations where the Post Office staff would collect them and sort them out for the various districts. This would happen all the way along the line from London to Glasgow.

In the 1960s, crooks decided to hijack one of the trains and collected over a million pounds, which in those days was an awful lot of money, even when compared with a £53,000,000 bank raid that took place in 2006. But in those days this was a sophisticated crime, taking the bags from the train and the money in them, straightaway. I believe after a year or two they found most of the villains that were involved in the crime except one elusive character, Ronnie Biggs. He managed to escape to Brazil and avoided capture for many years despite the valiant efforts of Jack Slipper of Scotland Yard.

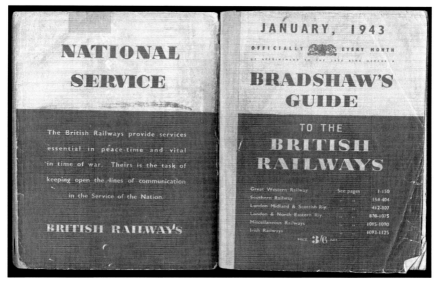

Bradshaw's Railway Guide

Despite this one, very famous, crime, the parcels service over the years has operated very smoothly and I think we owe a great deal of gratitude to the postal service and the railways for the service given. The other pre-War benefit we had from the railway service was the fact that you could buy a booklet called Bradshaw's Railway Timetable, a monthly publication that I used to receive at the office where I worked. It gave every station in the country, the times of arrival and departure and the current prices for first, second and third class travel. It was a great help to the train travelling public and affectionately known as the ABC although 'Bradshaw's' was the correct title. To be able to plot a route and know exactly how much it would cost, and the time the journey would take was a marvellous advantage to have for a business commuter like me.

Ten to twelve years after the Government nationalised the railways and the gradual process of taking over the main line railways and reducing the staff quota had taken place, certain sections of the organisation were handed over to private companies to run. Maintenance and Signal operations were treated in a different manner. It also took this long period of time before it was realised that the outlying stations dotted all around the country, in villages and in remote parts, were not profitable. Either they did not have enough people to transport or the goods that were going to and from that area were not earning sufficient money for them to make it possible to maintain the station; despite the fact that the main railways had managed the system adequately in the past. During this period the Government appointed a Dr Beeching to oversee the problem of the inefficient rail network and he found that they would all have to be axed to enable the establishment of a neater form of rail communication – that is all it was. They had always been subsidised by the main users, LNER, LMS, GW and Southern but when the Government took over, little regard or respect was given to the livelihood and happiness of the people living in these outlying villages. They then denuded a transport system that had been set up for them many, many years earlier, that they had all enjoyed; their fathers, grandfathers and grandmothers before; to wait for a train to go to visit someone or to work, to get a glimpse of what was happening in the towns and cities miles away from where they lived, had now been taken away from them. Dr Beeching's axe had fallen.

There were various protests; a vigorous one from the Lincolnshire area, which was a prosperous farming area in those days, which had great potential. That area was not far from the steel mills but Dr Beeching arranged for most of the small railways in Lincolnshire to be closed. There was a tremendous fight against this and I believe he had to give way eventually on some of the closures. Others fought but very few survived the axe, only here and there where they made their protest loud enough, or there was some incentive.

When the Railway Nationalisation Bill was passed in 1948, the London Passenger Transport Board became the London Transport Board, missing out the word 'Passenger', and this was very important as far as they were concerned because it was under their control. It had been running perfectly as the London Passenger Transport Board throughout the War period making a magnificent effort for the people who relied on getting to work on time from very long distances. The network of the Underground system covered many miles outside the London area and all round plus all the intricate railway schemes that were inside the Metropolis. The Central, Northern and Piccadilly lines and all the various lines that criss-crossed each other to serve districts in the centre of the Capital also linked up with those on the outskirts, all in all somewhere in the region of 200 square miles. In addition, many of the stations acted as underground shelters during the heavy bombing experienced from the Luftwaffe during the War. Some photographs of this are in my book, *Poplar at War*; one is of the platform at the Elephant and Castle showing people trying to get some rest away from the night time bombing.

Lucker Water Troughs
Copyright JW Armstrong Trust

John Hector

It took a long, long time to get the railways sorted out; even today, almost sixty years later, the four lines that are in control are privately owned and there are now various sections owning different parts of the network. It has been broken down until it has become the responsibility of not one but thousands of people. The charges for rail travel have become exorbitant and the system is used less and less for the transport of goods.

I would like to say thank you to the Darlington Railway Museum for being so helpful in loaning me the pictures, which have been reproduced in this book; to them my grateful thanks.

Steel Nationalisation

For ten years of my working life from 1931 to 1941 I was involved, very deeply, in the purchasing of steel for the manufacture of various types of equipment for a tank-producing company in Limehouse, East London; very near to the original launching spot of Brunel's iron ship, *The Great Eastern*. For the following ten years I was associated with a new company of stockholders called Brown and Tawse Ltd, originally founded in Dundee. They were well known throughout the country as being the leading stockholders of all purpose, black steel sheets, plates, girders and every type of steel required for the industry. The United Kingdom had the best reputation in the world for producing steel of all types. Scotland was well known throughout the world for shipbuilding. South Wales produced sheet steel, at the Richard Thomas and Baldwin works and the Steel Company of Wales; this sheet steel was then used in the production of motorcar bodies for Ford Motor Co, Morris Austin, Vauxhall and for various other manufacturers in the United Kingdom.

In the Midlands we had a whole host of firms that were 'steel re-rollers' that would roll a section of steel into any shape that was necessary. There were a number of small companies specialising in reducing oval steel from round bars, flats, angles and steel channels to all kinds of shapes and sizes, mainly very small sizes, nothing exceeding two inches.

John Hector

In the North East of England we had a girder producing company called Dormond Long which at one stage was commissioned to produce the massive girders needed for the Sydney Harbour Bridge, which were then shipped to Australia. The architect's instructions for these girders were that they should be started from each side of the Harbour and after many months of welding and riveting, came within an inch or two apart to connect in the middle, which was considered then a magnificent feat for which the company became renowned.

The pictures on the following pages show the great Dorman Long Works and the nearby South Durham Steel Works, which was very close to the famous Redcar race course; these, along with the Consett Iron Company and Jarrow Iron Works, were sites that I visited very many times.

Britannia Works 1947

After 1945

Outside shot of the works

The vast factory floor of the works

John Hector

Britannia Works interior

Aerial photo of Britannia Works

After 1945

In addition to the black steel industry that Brown and Tawse were involved in, I was thrust into the increasing manufacture of stainless steel, which had just begun at the start of the Second World War and was to expand greatly during the 1950s and 1960s.'

The steel produced throughout the United Kingdom was all manufactured to the same quality, which was called 'Siemens-Martin' (indeed, three-quarters of the World's production of iron and steel was produced to this standard); there was also a basic steel manufactured for cheaper production called the 'Bessemer Process'.

For the first fifty years of the Twentieth Century, which included three wars – the Boer War and the First and Second World Wars – there was a great demand for a tougher steel to withstand shrapnel, shell fire and in some cases bullets. Not many steel producers could manufacture the hardened steel that was necessary for that purpose. Some produced a plate steel lined with copper sheet which, although it had a limited purpose, was used extensively by us in the manufacture of the cabins on landing craft or Landing Craft Marines (LCMs) as they were known. My brother, Harry, wrote about one of these cabins where he waited for many hours before turning his LCM towards the beaches for the D Day Landing in Normandy. I always hoped that we might have helped to save the lives of him and his crew by this protective coating method, had he been using one of the Landing Craft that we produced. The copper coated steel was only produced by one company in this country, The Consett Iron Company, in Consett, County Durham under the name of Corten.

On the back of Wartime experiences came great demand for other qualities of steel and it finally spread into the stainless steel area which was then required for manufacturing goods associated with the food industry.

We pioneered the manufacture of stainless steel in this country in all its various forms. There was a company in Scunthorpe called 'Apple Frodingham', part of the 'United Steel Company', which purchased 'Samuel Fox' in Sheffield and together embarked on production of a wide range of stainless steel of every type. Another important stainless producer also from Sheffield was Firth Vickers, an off-shoot of the famous Vickers that produced guns, rifles and machine guns for the First and Second World Wars. They gained a high reputation for their finish and reliability throughout the World.

There was a great demand for stainless steel to suit all purposes. Some had to be very durable and have a long life; others had to be thin and ductile for the production of lightweight goods for use in the milk trade or for the beer industry. Both Vickers and Fox pioneered this method of manufacturing and each had success in different fields. Likewise there were many smaller companies in the Sheffield area that decided to specialise and started producing stainless steel in very small quantities, mainly in 'bar' form for which demand and prices were always high.

The variations in the qualities of the stainless steel were many; basically they were controlled by the elements that the steel contained and would resist certain chemicals and temperatures controlled by the nickel and molybdenum content. The finishes of the flat sheet and plate materials rolled were required to be either brush or, in most cases, highly polished surfaces. Very much later, Richard Thomas and Baldwin opened Llanwern Sheet mills some fifteen years after the other producers had made their in-roads into the trade for products which were now flooding the market. Brown and Tawse then extended their supply depots throughout the United Kingdom to cater for the high demands not only of stainless steel, but of course, for the wide range of tubes that were required for the American Petroleum Institute.

Referring to the demands for the motorcar industry that was now rapidly resuming production for the home and export markets, the designers found that the new markets required more modern and futuristic designs that would meet the demands of the enthusiastic purchasers. This became more apparent as their wealth started to increase in higher paid jobs and in the advancement of technology that left the old style flat cap workers well behind the higher class employees now being recruited by so many companies being listed on the Stock Exchange.

With the increase in competition in the steel distribution trade my life altered considerably as I was then forced to travel to every steel works and small 're-rollers' throughout the United Kingdom and through the mass of works in the Birmingham and Midland areas.

Fortunately, my buying power was extremely welcome wherever I went because cash payments by Brown and Tawse were always on the dot and many times I could press for a rebate or discount of two and a half per cent, or sometimes a five per cent allowance for a seven day prompt payment if I found that some of the smaller companies were pressed in the financial area. This discount when collected over our financial year resulted in a considerable sum.

In my thirtieth year of trading I received a shock when I was told on the grapevine that the new Labour Government, under Wilson, had decided to nationalise steel. The first British Steel Corporation was launched and entered on the government books in 1967, although it was some seventeen years before full acquisition took place in 1984. In the process of this period of purchase, I listened to the very many views of steel producers. They all had the uncomfortable realisation that their century-old method of iron and steel production was to be governed by teams of bureaucrats, who had very little knowledge of the workings of the manufacturers. Their need was for good, safe, reliable supplies of steel in all its forms to carry on their production, whether it was for cars or any of a variety of products needed throughout the UK.

Ultimately it was found that the Ford motor company and others required wider and more ductile sheets from suppliers in Holland and large tonnages were imported to satisfy the new designs. This proved a great loss to the British sheet steel industry.

In the seventeen years from its inception to the final takeover date in 1984 we witnessed the procrastination of the Government with its short-sighted view of the steel industry's value. Overseas production increased in Germany, with its newly formed steel industries, Krupps and Manheim (both these mills had been financed with the aid of the American Marshall plan), the stainless steel works in Sweden came into operation and the widely growing, fast flowing, steel producers emerged in Japan. The latter cut a wide angle of price reduction in the stainless steel sheet trade which seriously affected the traditional trading of the United Kingdom. As this country's mills had not expanded or modernised and in most cases were being run down and closed as the Government found that time had caught up with them, the overseas suppliers developed their markets. There were millions of workers employed in so many countries, anxious to find work, and so they accepted lower wages, far lower than those paid by the British steel masters, i.e. the new British Steel Corporation.

Before signing off on this chapter I wish to record that I saw so many changes in the customers' demands for steel. One of the earliest recollections was supplying the markets of China with four-inch cut nails in half hundred-weight bags, each with a wooden label indicating the contents and number. These were supplied to the paddy field owners and were placed nearby the stem to revitalise the earth as the rusting steel saturated the ground that had been used to grow rice stems, in some cases, for centuries.

Following on, I remember tracking supplies of equipment necessary for the tube expanding mechanism of the earliest jet propelled aircraft, The Comet, which exploded in the Mediterranean on one of its early test flights. Prior to my many years at Brown and Tawse, we traded with many overseas underdeveloped countries through our London Wall Office and large quantities of reinforcing steel wire and rods were supplied to help them produce reinforced concrete buildings. Ultimately, we supplied them with part of the machinery necessary for them to produce their own reinforced wire from scrap iron that they imported from other countries in exchange for native grown products which they had in abundance. Looking back we had helped some countries to survive and others to act as competitors to us when they found that they were producing

After 1945

more than they needed and undercut our prices to their next-door neighbour.

In 1974 it was a sad day when I retired from my job as chief buyer and had to say goodbye to so many wonderful and knowledgeable men who had nursed the steel industry, in some cases through three wars, and had brought British shipbuilding to the fore from Brunel's period to the latest Atlantic luxury liners such as the Queen Mary; as well as the hundreds of cargo and oil tankers that were produced on the Clyde, the Tyne, the Tees and not forgetting the Tay.

Sadly, in 1999, the British Steel Corporation ceased to exist as it had been absorbed by the Dutch Company, Corus, who still maintain a small share of the celebrated British Steel Industry after the closure of so many unprofitable mills. Now in the year 2007 there are only a few mills working full time in the United Kingdom.

The most prominent company that remains in my mind and must be mentioned in full with my gratitude for the great help they gave to Brown and Tawse Ltd, was Colvilles, West George Street, Glasgow. They were skilled in producing many types of steel from plates to girders, round bars and later steel strip in sheet form at the Ravenscraig Mills. I had many friends amongst the workforce at the various Colville Works, including West George Street, Clydesbridge, Coatbridge, Govan and the Daziel Mills.

The personnel at all these establishments were most kind to me throughout the thirty years that I dealt with them and I well remember the excellent luncheons they laid on for me during my visits, especially the festive table that was set up to be enjoyed after the disappearance of the company Chairman so that we could enjoy the Scotch, beer and wine so liberally available, hidden whilst he was present, he being well known for his abstinence!

The Chairman and Directors of Brown and Tawse were also associated in other financial fields such as the Caledon Shipbuilding concern and other Scottish industries including canister manufacturing. These additional interests I learned about

John Hector

over the many years of visiting my friends whilst searching for numerous products, a lot of which were in very short supply, but I always came away with promises that were honoured; my heartfelt thanks for all the assistance.

Thanks to Teesside Archives and the Friends of Teesside Archives for the work in compiling these photographs and to Corus for permission to use the images of Dorman Long Britannia Works.

Looking north towards St. Leonard's Street (left) and Bow Road immediately above the railway bridge over the Lea. Nicholson's Distillery (right); Kemball, Bishop and Co. (centre); Brown & Tawse Ltd (bottom left, adjoining the railway) 1962.

The Docks

The severe damage to the major docks that occurred during the bombing raids of 1940 to 1944 meant that the whole of the River Thames' docking facilities suffered to such an extent that cargo ships from all over the world were diverted to Liverpool and Glasgow. The loss of equipment, cranes, wharfage, quays and warehouses to the Royal Albert, West and East India, Millwall and Surrey Commercial docks was considerable. The area that these docks covered from Woolwich to the City of London became unusable throughout the War period.

Tower Bridge and Pool of London

Our grateful thanks to www.eastlondonpostcards.co.uk for the images of London docks.

Port of London

Royal Docks

The docks were the main source of employment for a large percentage of the population of Poplar, Stepney, Millwall, Canning Town and West Ham.

After 1945

Millwall Docks

When the service men returned to their homes around the various docks they were amazed to see the extent of the damage that had occurred. Quite a lot of repair work was done between 1943 and 1945 but in the interim they found that most of the shipping lines had rearranged their routes and never again would they come up the Thames to unload or collect their cargoes for further distribution throughout the world. The loss of the docks and traffic gave additional problems to the vast number of men employed, pre-War, as dockers, stevedores, crane drivers, tally clerks and haulage contractors.

In the course of time the various councils that held the docks in their perimeter found that they were costing too much money to service on a falling market. After a lot of thought, Southampton and Tilbury, whose docks had been maintained and repaired speedily, were thought to offer efficient working arrangements. Latterly it would be accepted that both Southampton and Tilbury were the nearest ports in the British Isles to accept container vessels and dock workers there would learn the new skill of unloading and stacking these huge containers.

Hundreds of stevedores, dockers, crane drivers and checkers were dispatched to Southampton and Tilbury from the East London

John Hector

area and this caused considerable upheaval in the dock employment in both of these areas, when hundreds and eventually thousands of workers descended on their docks from East London.

Although the Port of London Authority patched up several of the docks with emergency repairs, the cargo trade for import and export had gained hold throughout the world and the cargo ships that ventured up the Thames required a minimum amount of labour in each dock that accepted these cargo vessels. In fact, the East London Dock closed down completely in1951 but the Royal Albert and Victoria Docks carried on until the early 1980s until they, too, were closed.

Eventually it proved necessary to inform the various unions, The Stevedores' Union and the Dock Workers' Unions, that the services of their members were no longer required and a certain amount of redundancy was, eventually, paid to those who had spent a lifetime in the local employment of dock handling and dock cargo handling. Redundancy pay in those days was minute and based on pre-War levels, whereas the amount now received has to be paid against a high cost of living as the inflation rate has climbed dramatically.

This resulted in a swelling of unemployment in the Dockland areas that lastedwell into the 1950s and the population began moving out of the docks because no re-housing was taking place in the area. The docks themselves became widely disused and ultimately sold off as various housing complexes. At present, these properties are valued at enormous amounts of money for purchase by high earning City workers in the Stock Exchange, Banking and Insurance industries that flourish in London. High rise buildings, for example the enormous Canary Wharf, is a case in point of the development of the new 'Docklands' area.

The advanced use of container vessels became widespread throughout the world and, post-War, nine of our ports, throughout the United Kingdom, were obliged to equip with the machinery necessary for handling the cargoes within the containers. The design of these large vessels has been so immense that we found,

After 1945

in the year 2006, the arrival off the East Coast, at Harwich, a large container vessel from China (not hitherto known as a maritime trader), reputed to be as long as five football pitches. The cargo in the containers held a multiplicity of goods that were cheaply manufactured and are now being distributed throughout the world, upsetting many traditional markets with their low cost imports.

Kind acknowledgements to Philip Cone for the loan of the following photographs:

The Colchester *(1971) after being newly lengthened in 1969 for conversion to a ceullular container ship to replace the* Isle of Ely *on the Rotterdam run.*

Dart Americana *and* Dart Europe *working cargo at the newly completed Walton Container Terminal, Felixstowe*

Clean Air

At the end of March 1947 and throughout the most severe winter conditions, there was a shortage of coal due to non-production across the United Kingdom, and the large stocks that had been dispatched remained frozen in transit. Householders were forced to rely on candles and oil lamps and what timber could be found to heat the stoves for warmth and food. This was a blessing in disguise because the atmosphere that the Arctic conditions produced was the cleanest air that we had ever had in the country where no fossilised fuel was being used, domestically or industrially. Now, sixty years on, 'Global Warming' is our biggest problem, discovered as a result of the high pollution of our air space due to transport on roads and in the air. The Clean Air Act, intended to reduce the soot laden era in our cities, is now a must for our future.

Before the War, East London was plagued with fog during most winters and the soot from thousands of terraced houses and factory chimneys combined to form a smog-like atmosphere. Being so close to the Rivers Thames and Lea and the two canals, the Grand Union and the Prince Regent that ran across the area, made the streets fog-bound for days on end. A good strong wind was the only salvation for families anxious to get the washing done and on the clothes line, thus avoiding them having to dry the wet washing in the rooms fuelled by the cooking stoves constantly on the go and filling the streets with smoke.

After 1945

In London, when the bombed sites were cleared of the millions of tons of rubble carted away to the landfill sites around the Capital, the wonderful old buildings that were centuries old were exposed, showing the soot laden brick and stone work with thick deposits, which, when soaked with rain, set up an acid type liquid that eroded the excellent carvings that had been carried out by so many skilled craftsmen hundreds of years before.

The Clean Air Act came before Parliament and helped people move away from coal fire cooking and converting to gas and electricity for cooking and heating. The factories became more modernised and moved out of London to much cheaper sites.

Kind acknowledgements to Tower Hamlets Library for the following two photographs:

War time debris on the site of Thistle House and Heather House, Brunswick Road 1955

John Hector

Factory chimneys

Kind acknowledgements to Clacton Library for the following photograph:

*The Great London smog of 1952
(from internet website: www.portfolio.MVM.ed.ac.uk)*

After 1945

Then came the birth of smokeless fuel, a great improvement on home heating for a cosy fire. With the widening of new thoroughfares and walkways between some of the historic buildings in the city and West End, London was given an atmospheric new look. A widespread effort was then made to clean lots of the historic buildings restoring them to their former beauty. This was part of the new scheme to de-scale the soot and grime from the outsides of well known buildings such as St Paul's Cathedral and other historic landmarks, Mansion house, Westminster Abbey, The Bank of England and Big Ben. These renovated buildings nestled in to the new architect designed tower buildings such as Canary Wharf, the Post Office Tower and the new Stock Exchange and gave overseas visitors a 'then and now' aspect of London, modernised after the attempt by the Nazis to invade our island.

Soon after the Clean Air Act came into force we saw the demise of the huge gasometers that adorned our cities from the Victorian era. These huge tank-like reservoirs supplied coal gas through gas meters to households when coins were inserted into the slot. This was a sort of 'pay as you use' or burn arrangement.

Large areas, that housed the gas works, as we called the yards, produced the gas from the retort house which extracted gas from ships and the train loads of coal that arrived daily, ensuring supplies would always be available. Many other products would be extracted from the coal and the residue would end up as coke, in itself a smokeless fuel. This valuable heat source was cheaper to use as a fuel, but of course it was less powerful.

The first stage of the demise of the gas holders was the discovery of methane gas from oil refining. Large ships were constructed and at Canvey Island, Essex, pits were dug to store the gas in sub-zero temperatures. It was then drawn off to various pumping stations and piped to the customers after treatment for safety aspects. This method was then made obsolete in the 1970s when natural gas was discovered in the North Sea. A large recovery depot was set up at Bacton on the East coast for gas distribution through a network of pipes throughout the UK. Today, many countries are supplying us

John Hector

at various levels of prices and gone is the pungent smell of old coal gas that was always prominent in the air when the gas works were working or in the house if the jet was not ignited properly. Gone, too, were the famous gas companies; 'The Gas Light and Coke Company,' 'Commercial Gas' and 'South Suburban Gas'. The cookers, fires and other appliances they hired, sold or otherwise provided can still be seen in various museums in cities throughout the UK, showing the things our mothers and grandmothers had to put up with in days gone by. One gas holder is preserved at the 'Oval Cricket Ground' in Vauxhall, South London and can be seen regularly on TV.

The Festival of Britain

In May 1951 the Festival of Britain was opened. It was to be a 'Tonic for the Nation' after the deprivations of War, to give a feeling of recovery and progress. The Labour Deputy Leader, Herbert Morrison, had the vision three years before to organise a team of young, energetic representatives from all creative fields to begin work on buildings on the South Bank of the River Thames.

We in the South of England were looking forward to the creation of the Festival Hall and the completion of the Exhibition itself with the South Bank Walk and the Battersea Funfair and its promise of fun for both adults and children alike, and the newspaper reports eagerly followed the progress.

Daily Mail *front page 1951*

John Hector

The Royal Festival Hall (1951) showing the completed building and Shot Tower from across the River Thames

It was to be a celebration to mark the 100th anniversary of the Great Exhibition of 1851 that had taken place at Crystal Palace and once more it was to be a showcase for all that was good about Britain. Buildings such as the Skylon, an unusual cigar shaped building, the Dome of Discovery and the Festival Hall all quickly took shape. The Lion and the Unicorn Pavilion housed a celebration of British History, aimed at promoting the very best in British art with works by both Henry Moore and Barbara Hepworth, and in design, technology and industry. The Festival proved to be very popular with London centre pieces including the South Bank Exhibition and the Festival Gardens in Battersea and the Battersea Park Funfair which attracted many thousands of visitors. Cities and villages nationwide all took part in the Festival and by September 1951 eighteen million people had joined in the Festival of Britain.

After 1945

The Royal Festival Hall (1951) west and front elevations

The Festival Gardens (1956) Battersea Park

John Hector

Naturally, the project was not without its critics who argued that the vast amount of money spent on the Festival would be better used to build houses. A plan was devised to build a large housing estate as part of the Festival in the borough of Poplar to celebrate the wonderful work of George Lansbury who died in 1940. He had been a tireless campaigner for the poor and underprivileged of the area and was so committed to the cause of unfair rates levied on the poorest families and the Government's lack of feeling for the welfare of the poor of the borough that he and several other councillors were jailed because of their defiance. The estate unfortunately was not particularly well thought out or attractive and covered a large part of the East End, incorporating part of the famous Chrisp Street Market. The original market was over a mile and a half long and was a thriving community of shops and stalls and side roads that had additional markets tacked on to them to spider its way across the East End. However, this market was shortened to twenty or so shops when it crossed the new 'Lansbury Estate' and was renamed the 'Lansbury Market', but the atmosphere changed. Herbert Morrison promoted the use of Lansbury's name as he had known George Lansbury when Morrison had been Mayor of Bethnal Green during the time of Lansbury's imprisonment. Earlier, Lansbury had invited Morrison to join him in his stand against Government but Morrison had declined and Poplar was out on its own. It is thought that Morrison felt he owed Lansbury a debt of gratitude for those times and a lasting recognition of Lansbury's work. The estate is still in existence unlike many of the buildings which were hastily cleared soon after the end of the Festival as the then Labour Government had lost power and the incoming Conservatives probably saw the exercise as political revenge.

With all the impressive attractions of the Festival of Britain on offer it was a marvellous boost to trade and tourism, which was exactly the original intention. It was hoped that the Millennium Dome would echo the same success for Britain in the year 2000 especially as (on a more whimsical note) the Grandson of Herbert Morrison, Peter Mandelson, was an advocate for the Dome's inception.

Latterly the Festival was seen as the unfulfilled promise of post-War Britain but the Festival generated a profit with which the Greater London Council converted the Royal Festival Hall and established the South Bank, and gave many benefits to the population in the way of lasting memories of a Great Britain, proving that not everything can be measured in monetary terms.

Thanks and gratitude for the efficient service is extended to The London Metropolitan Archives for the photographs of the Festival Hall and the Festival Gardens.

Gambling

After the War the public were generally inclined to try and better themselves, to escape the pre-War poverty that existed with the depression in the early 1930s. Gambling was one way to see if they could get a better living and more money in their pocket, either by a weekly flutter on the football pools or by other methods.

Just prior to the Second World War football pools were beginning to take shape. Littlewoods and Vernons claimed the market by introducing regular weekly coupons sent by post with addressed envelopes enclosed for you to return the forecast you made together with the appropriate postal order for the exact amount. The most popular bet on both coupons was four 'aways' (that meant four teams had to win away from home), three draws and ten results where you had to forecast the result of ten matches out of the given number on the coupon. Then the most popular one of all was the points system on which you had to make a claim if you could make eight draws, which would give you a maximum of twenty-four points; three points for a draw, two for an away win and one point for a home win. The idea was to post the coupon well in advance for Wednesday to make sure that it would arrive on time in Liverpool, which was the main distribution point for football pools companies.

After the War Zetters pools opened in London and they reduced their 'points' entries from a penny to a halfpenny per entry,

After 1945

thereby enabling the punters to increase their number of chances but the winnings were reduced. The number of people who bet on Zetters was very small compared with the hundreds of thousands of clients on the two major companies. The results were always eagerly awaited every Saturday. During the War, football pools stopped because of the question of postage time which would never be reached and of course most matches were called off because of the lack of support, because of the male population serving in the War. Of course, to muster large crowds to watch would have been hazardous in the time of enemy action; so the football pools were virtually stopped from 1939 to the 1944/45 period. When they opened up once more people found that they would like to venture an extra few shillings per week on the football pools because the money was a little bit more plentiful and the chance of a good bonus win was very motivating. One would dream before the War of such prizes as a new motorcar, caravan holiday, the purchase of a caravan and so on. Even, in some cases, the purchase of a new house, so it was a good gamble for them to venture on football pool wins.

From '66 to 2006 betting slips

We are grateful to Ladbrokes for supplying 'then and now' betting slips to illustrate this section.

Both the major companies set out on the coupons the number of points for matches that they thought would be more controversial and more difficult to forecast. Each company had the same number of players and matches being played and it was the punter's job to sort out the ways to win their forecast of a home, away or a draw. On Saturday evening at the end of most matches, the BBC would read out the football match scores with their indication of a home win, away or draw so that you could easily pick out whether your bet had won. At the end of the forecast when they gave the results they would then give the result of the information from Liverpool – whether the away wins would be a low or medium payout or if the draws would be either high or low – and they gave the punters throughout the country an indication of the possibility of a good or medium win, which heartened quite a number of people until they could get their end result, which would be published on Wednesday morning in the newspaper followed by postal order or cheque from Vernons or Littlewoods in the first post, also on the Wednesday of the published result.

In 1947 I was fortunate enough to win second place in the 'point's pool', a sum of £439, five shillings and nine pence. This set my bank balance up for many years.

It was some sixteen years after the War before the gambling public got their wish to bet in high street shops rather than participate in betting with street bookmakers who were continually harassed by the police. Arrests were forever being made of the bookmakers, their runners and anyone else involved in the betting fraternity that was carried out on the streets. Along the racecourses, betting was permitted and the nobility and all race goers could bet as much as they liked without question. The bookmakers would be waiting on the other side of the entrance to take on any bets that the punters may have. The trusted Tattersalls betting organisation, which was controlled from an office, took bets that were firmly laid, many on credit from recognised banking accounts. However, stories have been written about some bookmakers who disappeared before the end of the last race. When the punters went to look for the holders

After 1945

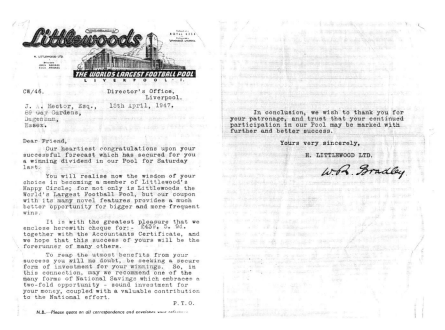

Copy of Littlewoods Football Pool letter showing the author's grand win in 1947

Copy of the Pools results for the winning draw

of their bets to collect the results of their winnings, they found that these unscrupulous types had long since disappeared from the course leaving the punters high and dry. The abolition of the street bookmakers that had been running, in most cases, for many years came about because of the introduction of legalised betting, the opening of high street betting shops and of course the levying of a betting tax.

Gambling was given official recognition in May 1961 and it was found that a more advantageous way for people to try and win large sums was either on the football pools or by placing large bets such as accumulators on which you could win fantastic amounts of prize money; if you were prepared to make a series of gambles. In this situation, we had a pre-War method of street bookmakers whereby the results of the horse races were not known until early evening when the newspapers brought the results to the shops. Today, with advanced technology, you are shown on TV the horses running, with the winners declared immediately and the bookmakers paying the winnings in a matter of minutes. Shops such as Ladbrokes and Corals opened up and gave the public up-to-the-minute information where you could study and see your fortune come and go out of the window, by standing in the shop and putting the money on the counter such as you do in the supermarkets.

During the 1930s we had the forerunner of the National Lottery from our bookmakers in the form of 'The Irish Hospitals Sweepstake'. We now have Lottery tickets and scratch cards, which are regularly purchased in the effort to obtain large sums to give us many of the delights that we expect of life. Unfortunately many big winners will not enjoy the life of luxury that they have pursued for years and we do read tragic stories of how large sums of money can upset family arrangements and lifetimes of love and devotion to their loved ones. Not all families enjoy wealth when it is not earned by hard work or bequeathed to them by their loved ones.

To sum up this chapter, for the last sixty years since the War, gambling has increased throughout the UK and throughout the world. It has brought tragedies, robberies, disruption to life and taken away many of the quieter aspects we enjoyed when we were poorer. Overall the Government, in giving the public more freedom to do as they please, have earned huge sums of money on entertainment tax, income tax and inheritance tax that has resulted from the public betting in whatever the chosen direction. Are we better off, when each Saturday night we now find television shows offering us million pound prizes for an evening's entertainment? Does it satisfy the gambling lust that we have inherited over the last sixty years?

Fully televised racing action

Grateful thanks to William Hill for providing this interior shot of one of their offices.

Holidays

From 1900, holidays for families in the south of England were limited to a short stay with aunts, uncles or grandmothers who lived near the sea. Boarding houses would not be in evidence until the early to mid-1930s and hotels were rarely used by ordinary folk.

In the north of England there was a special holiday period when the supposedly 'satanic mills' closed and Wakes Week took place. This annual closure enabled families to travel to Blackpool or the Yorkshire coast to enjoy the sight of the sea.

Beach holidays are always popular with some members of the family

After 1945

When the recession hit in the 1930s, it brought widespread unemployment and holidays were put on the back-burner for many people for several years. Then a period evolved in which holiday sites in major seaside towns were launched by Warners, Pontins, and Butlins. These companies offered a complete package deal of chalet, food, entertainment, free nursemaids for the children and first class entertainers to give a memorable holiday experience for the thousand or so residents spending their week at the camps. The camps proved exceedingly popular and made the coastal towns free for the casual visitors.

When the War started in 1939 the War Office gradually took over possession of these large sites with their chalet accommodation in various parts of the UK as they proved to be ideal billeting arrangements for the forces. The American army held on to the northern camps a long time after 1945 and the camp owners were well rewarded for the lengthened stay of the US forces.

Wartime meant there were no holidays at the seaside. In 1940 the threat of invasion from the continent by the Nazis meant that all the beaches on the west, south and east coast of England, and the Atlantic, English Channel and the North Sea coastlines were mined against possible invasion. Gradually the towns around these beaches became virtual ghost towns and many of the occupants moved back further away from the coast to avoid any clashes likely to be brought upon them by the enemy. Unfortunately these beaches were not cleared rapidly and it was not until the 1950s that the clearance of all beaches was formally announced by the Government. This made a return to normality a very slow process.

In the meantime the holiday camp owners ploughed ahead with rapid expansion and modernisation of all the camps to entice large numbers of people who now had more money and time to enjoy themselves after so many years of war weariness at the front or at home.

John Hector

Bathing pool and Cascade, Butlin's Holiday Camp, Clacton on Sea

Seaton Holiday Camp, Seaton, Devon

After 1945

Poolside fun at Butlin's Clacton on Sea, Essex

All entertainment was provided for within the camp

Our grateful thanks to The Clacton History Society for the loan of the photographs of Butlin's Holiday Camps.

Some of the entertainers at these camps went on later to become well known radio, film and television artists. Amongst some of the famous Redcoats were Jimmy Tarbuck, Des O'Connor, Cliff Richard and Roy Hudd, who was a Redcoat at the Clacton Butlins. Having cut their teeth performing to large, captive groups of people that had to be entertained nightly to high standards, it was a valuable proving ground. These folk enjoyed the privilege of wearing the 'blazer of honour' as a blue, green or red coat which characterised the company and camp that had promoted them.

Butlins of Clacton lay claim to the accolade of comfort, entertainment, cleanliness and service as being superior to the others.

People still enjoyed the simplicity of farmhouse accommodation holidays which once more started to prosper in the many valleys of rural England now that motor vehicles were beginning to find their way across England despite continuing petrol rationing.

Fine holidays were also planned and experienced by the lochs and mountains of Scotland and North Wales and here again more money was available from the savings of several years of thrift or money put aside for a 'sunny' day.

My family was fortunate enough to experience an 'overseas' holiday in 1948 to Jersey in the Channel Islands, which was provided by me from a £400 football pools second division win on the treble-chance that I had been doing for two years at thirty one-penny lines i.e., two and sixpence per week (now twelve pence). This holiday has given us a lifetime of memories in our photographic albums as the island we visited was still in the process of clearing up from the German occupation.

What came about next slowed the progress of all caravan and chalet camp holidays; cheap 'package' holidays abroad were being offered from the many aerodromes in the UK, which were now virtually unused. The facilities still existed and were available for accommodating and processing large numbers of people for return flights to many new foreign holiday destinations.

Later, our family was able to take advantage of some of these bargain holidays when the head of the typing pool at the office where I worked told me that her son was the manager of the Clarkson's Package Holiday Company that extensively advertised throughout the UK and had become the pioneer of low cost holidays abroad. Thousands of people turned to this method of holidaying and in many ways it was educational for children to know what other countries were like and for them to set their sights on future visits when they grew older.

Channel Islands airport (1948) - few holiday makers

Going abroad was the 'in-thing' to tell the neighbours when they enquired about your holiday arrangements. Spain, Greece, Italy and the Rhine were some of the countries that I visited due to cancelled opportunities that were telegraphed from the son to his mother in the office; the possibility of a £500 fortnight holiday being available for £120 for immediate acceptance that enabled the plane to be fully booked was too good an opportunity to miss.

John Hector

Over the twenty years from 1945 I took the advantage on four occasions to accept these holidays and the last one was a bargain trip to Sardinia with my daughter, Christine, and her husband and my wife enjoying the last of the Clarkson offers.

St. Brelades Bay, Jersey - the author and family

The holiday camps never recovered from the trend towards holidays abroad and local councils stepped in and purchased large areas of holiday camp land that was much needed for the building of new council estates in prime positions without the need to develop the surrounding area which had already taken place.

With the advent of new models of motorcars came the method of towing small caravans around the countryside for holidays. Soon a nationwide network of 'caravanners' was born, establishing many clubs, and the holidays became a method of 'getting away from it all' for the whole family.

Holidays would not be fully described if I failed to mention the many happy hours that were spent on houseboats moored on riverside sites and of cabin craft cruising the wide expanse of the Norfolk Broads and many other waterways in the United Kingdom. Sailing is popular not only for holidays but as a recreational hobby and is a regular pastime in all conditions.

Static caravan sites were wonderful holiday venues. Post-war 'towable' caravans saw a boom in popularity that continues today

Cars

As the buyer of Wartime supplies needed to keep the factory (Fraser and Fraser) going, it was very often put to me to try and obtain the unobtainable. Following the War my reputation had grown as being the man most able to locate whatever was needed. However, I was put to the test when the Secretary of the Company, who lived in Woodford, decided he would take over the company car that was being used by one of the engineers in the repair department. The car was a very tidy Ford Prefect and the Secretary used it regularly but he gave me the task of obtaining another car, preferably newer. Despite my protests that delivery of something so rare would be difficult as there was a two-year waiting list, he replied that "I should do whatever I could," and that he would "leave it to me."

Undaunted by the challenge I approached one of our suppliers who regularly serviced and maintained our lorries before and during the War. They said they would try to help and did we have any vehicle to part-exchange? Unfortunately I didn't, so I had to persuade one of the Directors to buy a new car without too much of a long wait. Not only did they have the new car but I was fortunate to be offered the Ford Prefect for my own use. It was a super little car and although I had taken out a driving licence during the War, I was only used to driving a three ton Bedford lorry during the emergency bombing. One rainy Friday evening the Secretary drove

After 1945

The shiny Ford Prefect

me over to the garage in Manor Park to collect the new car, handing over the Prefect to me during rush hour on a wet night. I waited for the traffic to ease for about half an hour and when finally, it did, I slowly set off on a journey home of ten miles with an ETA of thirty minutes at that time of night. Being extra careful, I drove in third gear holding the 'nippy' machine on the road and avoiding skids; bikes were even passing me at one time. One and a half hours later, I arrived home and had to remove the whole of the back gate and fence to allow the car into the bottom of the garden. In those days there were no garages or cars on the housing estate, lorries were the main means of transport and my car was much admired by all.

John Hector

I looked after my pride and joy really well, 'Simonising' (wax polishing) at every opportunity. It was my habit to park my Ford Prefect by the boardroom window near the directors' parking bays. It just so happened that one day during a managerial meeting the Chairman was looking out of the window and noticed my car. He enquired as to who owned the 1933, highly polished, Ford. When the Managing Director told him it was Jack Hector, the Chairman is reported to have said, "Any man that keeps an old car in such perfect condition deserves to be rewarded with a new vehicle". Angus, the MD, explained there would be a wait but he would see to it. I was told to go to Gates of Woodford to see a friend of Angus', a lady director of the garage and fellow churchgoer. I told her about the order through the company and we looked at some possible models. In the showroom was a Ford Consul that impressed me. The director explained it was a 'column change' with bench seating in the front which, in those days, was a rather comfortable option. I said I had a car to part-exchange and because it was in such good condition I was offered a remarkably high price. That's how I came to own my first new car, a green Ford Consul, ENO 804. I often wonder what happened to that car.

When Fraser and Fraser officially became part of Brown and Tawse my car was relinquished and I was allowed one of the 'pool' cars originally used by the representatives so that when I eventually owned the Austin A60, as the fleet cars were, it had been well used.

The car market opened up in the United Kingdom after the War because the Ministry of Supply stopped all contracts to supply the armed services, and manufacturers then found that they had to produce vehicles to suit the domestic market. Metal was still rationed very heavily and continued to be so well into the years after the War. Therefore the designs took into account the lack of raw materials as well as the suitability for family use. Even into the later years after the War most of the new designs were comparatively small in size with such brands as the Austin 8, Morris Minor and Ford Popular being market leaders.

After 1945

Ford Anglia

Other well-known brands included Wolseley, Riley, Rover and Sunbeam with the Talbot and Rapier models. The Ford Anglia and Ford Prefect were quite narrow vehicles, suitable for getting into most garages, and the lighter weight was appreciated for parking and easy access between premises with small driveways and courtyards where a vehicle could easily be parked. Into the 1960s came the iconic design by Issigonis for the Austin 7 / Morris 'Mini' Minor, distinguished only by different radiator grills and badges. This new concept of 'transverse axle' / front wheel drive vehicle was, latterly, successfully deployed in such models as the Allegro, Maestro and 11/13/1500 and 1800 which was also known as the 'land crab'. Badge 'engineering' became prominent with the manufacturers realising an MG badge on the humble 1300, plus luxury trim and some minor mechanical tinkering could greatly add to the vehicle's prestige; not to mention an enhanced profit margin.

The Hillman Imp and many other small vehicles came on to the market as it was necessary to have a price range to suit all pockets. Some larger vehicles were produced during the 1960s and 1970s such as the Morris Oxford and Austin Cambridge. These cars were for family use and the Morris Traveller, a design incorporating a lot of wood on the sides at the back of the bodywork, proved to be very popular as one of the first estate-type cars for larger families and useful for consigning equipment. Cars with roomy boot spaces often doubled as utility vehicles for carrying not only equipment but workmen and tools to sites.

Mini (1963)

Unfortunately, we lost quite a number of companies over the years. Some discontinued manufacturing for a number of reasons including the higher costs of production or they had either been taken over or left to neglect. Others had no new designs to look forward to for production in an unknown market. It was virtually left to Vauxhall, Ford, Austin and Morris that merged with BMC (British Motor Company) and latterly British Leyland to claim most of the market. In the early 1960s we then saw the French with their Peugeots and Renaults, the Germans with their Volkswagens, Italians with their Fiats and the Swedes with their Volvos come on

After 1945

to the market and supply many vehicles of different types, which again eroded part of the standard market. Until then, all our car production was manufactured in the UK and it was felt that their security was guaranteed, without much competition. In later years this was proved not to be the case, and despite the Government requesting the nation to back British brands, the market began to erode when the Japanese really began to manufacture and flooded the UK market with low cost, reliable vehicles.

MG 1100 (1968)

Early 70s Triumph

The News and BBC Radio

1946 was a memorable year for thousands of radio listeners, as it was the beginning of two much loved BBC Radio Programmes; 'Woman's Hour' (now in its 61st year) and 'Down Your Way'.

'Woman's Hour' is still with us today, more modernised from the original format which was broadcast at different times during the day, as and when it could be slotted in. It started life as a listener's request show for a favourite tune to be played on a 78 rpm record which, at that time, was the only type available. Christopher Stone, the well loved presenter, initially chaired the programme, starting off with the signature tune, 'Greensleeves', which the listeners had chosen by vote. The BBC had its critics in the newly elected Labour Government with some of the recently elected MPs suggesting that women should be doing the housework or looking after the children rather than listening to a specially devised radio show. Some even objected to a listener's choice of a well known popular song by the Jewish singer Issie Bonn entitled 'Thanks for the Lovely Weekend' as being too suggestive!

Criticism aside, 'Woman's Hour' became so popular it was given a regular mid-morning broadcasting time that later became early afternoon and stayed that way until 1991 when Michael Green bravely moved the time to between ten and eleven a.m. on weekdays. There was a huge outcry; even the Queen asked why the programme had been moved. 'Woman's Hour' remains one of the best loved programmes on Radio 4 and over the years has been hosted by various presenters, some of whom have become legends to the more senior listeners. Jean Metcalfe, presenter from 1947 to 1958, remembers guests arriving for interviews wearing hats; Marjorie Anderson, Jenni Murray and Sue MacGregor are all household names; the present day's presenter is Martha Kearney. The subjects may have changed over the years but the original idea of discussing and airing views on a wide variety of topics has remained and the programme has consistently moved with the times, pioneering the art of cutting edge, radio journalism.

Windup record player for 78s

John Hector

50s/60s autochange record players, play 45, 33 and 78 rpm records.

'Down your way' was first aired on a Sunday afternoon, hosted by a well known sports reporter from Canada named Stewart McPherson who held the chair for about two years before returning to sports commentating. He was then replaced by the lovely wartime reporter Richard Dimbleby who ran the show from 1950 to 1955. Dimbleby, in his memoirs, reported that he had stayed in over a hundred hotels and travelled thousands of miles throughout his career whilst presenting 'Down Your Way', which was recorded throughout the United Kingdom.

After 1945

The programme was based on research from various town councils giving the producers details of local inhabitants and characters with interesting stories to tell. Usually eight to ten people would be interviewed on air for a short time each week with an amusing or interesting story to tell. Editing must have been quite an art form, because, as with all things, occasionally, things went wrong.

It is said that on one occasion the reporter knocked at the door of a bewildered couple's house who, nonetheless, made him very welcome. It was not until later that he found out he had visited the wrong address. The farm labourer and his wife were quite happy to let this man with a microphone join them for Sunday lunch and acted as though it was an everyday occurrence. The genuine interviewees were anxiously awaiting the BBC man some miles further on down the road! Apologies were offered all round and this error was never repeated again in the lifetime of the show.

After Richard Dimbleby, several other reporters followed until finally Brian Johnson, the famous Test Match commentator, ended the series with a final farewell tribute.

'Woman's Hour' and 'Down Your Way' were only on the air for a short time from August 1946 until early December of that year when the worst winter for a hundred years began and the Government decreed a shut down of vital services to conserve power. The BBC could only broadcast for a few hours to give vital news information. Both of these programmes suffered a shut down until April 1947.

Radio broadcasting gave the British public a wonderful legacy of talent. Most families owned a radio and each evening they settled down in the living room to listen to their favourite entertainers – Tommy Handley and the 'Itma' (It's that man again) Show, Elsie and Doris Waters, the gossiping neighbours, Rob Wilton with his catchphrase 'The Day the War broke out' or the Western Brothers with their cultural discussions on topics of note. One curiously-named comedy act was 'Stainless Stephen', so named because he hailed from Sheffield, home of much of the country's stainless steel production. We have come a long way with today's technology giving us the 'digital' clarity of sound on our radios but in those early days the pioneering radio broadcasts were infinitely more exciting.

News Theatres

After the War we found that the lovely little News Theatres that had kept us so well informed throughout the last twenty years were gradually closing. The informative newsreels that were broadcast were widely respected for their reliability in delivering authentic stories. The News Theatres were very useful entertainment halls and were located in most major cities, often adjacent to main line railway stations. They provided the public with an ideal opportunity to sit for an hour or so in comfort whilst waiting for their next train. Regular cinema-goers were used to having a newsreel preceding the main feature film. To watch the action that covered the news stories previously heard on the radio was an important part of the programme.

Primarily the News Theatres were established to keep the public informed of the stories behind the headlines. National and sporting events, where coverage could be planned in advance, were eagerly awaited but the standard fare of newsreel film shown on a daily basis was interspersed with cartoons, film 'shorts' and travelogues. Each programme was devised to last two hours and was run on a continuous loop with only the occasional interlude. Prices for the two hours (or more as there was no obligation to leave and many enjoyed a good nap in the comfortable seats!) ranged from one shilling to one shilling and sixpence. In those days there were no anti-smoking laws and the practice was encouraged with a five o'clock interlude for the usherettes to come round and empty the overflowing ashtrays. With the Theatres open from ten a.m. until eleven p.m., very often the interiors took on an atmosphere reminiscent of a bar room with the air laced with pipe, cigarette and cigar smoke and alcohol. Occasional intermissions gave the opportunity to purchase ice cream and 'Butterkist' popcorn as well as cigarettes from the kiosk in the foyer or via the usherette's tray.

Negative No: H23033 - Foyer of the Monseigneur News Theatre, London

Negative No: D18317 - US Servicemen walking past the Monseigneur News Theatre

After 1945

The news content of the two hour programme was supplied by Pathé, British Movietone or Gaumont British (whose catchphrase was "The eyes and ears of the World") and voice-over commentaries were usually made by the distinctive tones of the well known Bob Danvers-Walker or Leslie Mitchell, both BBC announcers. Obligatory in the showing would be an advertising slot; usually 'Pearl and Dean' who filmed local companies in return for a fee and free admission to the theatre as a perk. Standard advertisers would always make an appearance such as 'Aspro' or J. Collis Browne.

The marvellous service these theatres provided was much appreciated especially for coverage of events of national importance; for instance, Neville Chamberlain's 'Peace in our Time' paper waving at Croydon airport and the Coronation of Queen Elizabeth in June 1953.

The special newsreel on show is the film of the 1953 Coronation of Queen Elizabeth II.
Courtesy Leeds City Museum.

John Hector

There were no trailers for the next week's movies and as the shows were on a continuous loop you were always guaranteed to catch up with your favourite cartoons ranging from 'Popeye' with his amazing spinach, 'Tom and Jerry' escapades and the 'Three Stooges' (Curly, Larry and Mo). A ten minute dance band feature provided a welcome break too.

For whatever purpose the individual user of the News Theatres intended, be it for education, shelter, amusement or even a clandestine meeting place; the theatres were an interesting part of our cinematic history and it was sad to witness their gradual closure. Many of them were on prime sites, near to main line stations and so they were valuable to post-War development and so the Great British public were, once more, confined to the dreary waiting rooms on station platforms.

Photographs courtesy of the Imperial War Museum, London.

National Service

During the Second World War the 'Mobility Act' came into being, which enforced an Act of Parliament that stated that men over the age of eighteen would be liable to be 'drafted' into active service for their country, apart from those who were in 'Reserved Occupations'. These included, of course, the Army, armament makers, Doctors and Police, bus drivers, train drivers, farmers and a whole host of essential workers that kept the country going during the War.

There were exemptions, too, if men and boys were chosen to work down the coalmines. Many existing miners had been called up to fight in the War and the shortfall was made up of conscripts being sent to work in the mines rather than join one of the services. This selection was devised by a ballot scheme set up by the then Minister of Labour, Ernest Bevin, earning the thousands of young men, picked this way to work in the mines, the nickname of 'Bevin Boys'. Theirs was a largely forgotten part of the vital War effort and it is only now, some sixty years on, that their hard work has the recognition it so rightly deserves. Some who were 'Bevin Boys' later went on to become household names such as Brian Rix, Eric Morecambe and Jimmy Savile.

The 'Mobility Act' was, once more, brought to the fore in 1947 when it was suggested that men aged eighteen and over could be 'called up' for eighteen months' active service and

John Hector

'reserved' for a further four years. These National Servicemen would have the choice of the three services; Army, Navy or the Air force. The Act was enforced in 1948 and the men called up were deployed for training throughout the country in their chosen service. Most, however, went into the Army as, although Europe was now at peace, throughout the World there was still an immense amount of fighting taking place in different areas. The United Nations was now the world's peace-keeping force, making sure that any trouble was dealt with quickly by sending in troops from different countries to quell any fighting. Britain, for her part, was looking after her 'Empire'; the Crown Colony of Hong Kong and various regions in Africa were all guarded against possible trouble. We needed a fighting force to step in at a moment's notice to protect areas of possible tension and guard the population.

For my part, although I had been crippled from birth, during the War I was called up at the age of twenty for an examination in Ilford, and they classified me as being 'C3'. Despite having a job in what was a reserved occupation, making equipment for the armed services, I was considered, as a 'C3', able to be enlisted, should the need arise. It was annoying to me that my firm did not register me as 'reserved' although I believe they did not consider I would ever be asked to fight.

I felt both sadness and annoyance when the 'Mobility Act' came into being at the end of the War, when mothers that had watched their sons and husbands go off to War, now had to witness their younger sons of eighteen, whom they had nurtured throughout their school years during the War, go off to fight unknown enemies with the UN forces. Fortunately, we had a well trained Army with a residue of many servicemen that had been through the War and were not 'demobbed' and thus available to fight alongside the newly enlisted, wherever needed, around the world.

In 1951, my son-in-law, George Stovell, was a new recruit enlisted into the army under the Mobility Act. He was just eighteen and his mother had already lost his brother during the War whilst he had been serving on the submarines; his body was never recovered. Now to be told her other son was to be sent to fight, somewhere in what should be peacetime was a cruel blow. George was sent to Aldershot for initial training and then drafted into the Suffolk regiment for eventual posting overseas. He was immediately sent out to Malaya to fight the Communist rebels that were in the jungle and making life very unpleasant for the population, causing a big problem for the Malayan government. When George arrived he was attached to 'A' Company of the Suffolk Regiment, which had just completed, with other nations, over a year's tour of duty in Korea under the guidance of the UN, to quell the fighting between North and South. With a peace proposal taking shape, the various armies were deployed elsewhere and the Suffolk Regiment took their post in Malaya. With the training he received in Aldershot, George was now expected to go into jungle combat with his issue of lethal weapons on a kill-or-be-killed basis. Reflecting on this situation now it must have been a truly awful experience for not only the young men involved but for their mothers, girlfriends, wives and family to go through. To have endured the War and all its hardships and suffering and to now have peacetime but not be allowed to enjoy the experience because part of the family had been drafted, yet again, into a war.

I contacted the Suffolk Regiment in Bury St Edmunds as George had said that a number of personnel had died at the rebels' hands, and the archivist confirmed that eleven members of the Company had died. Fortunately my son-in-law survived but what a dreadful experience for him to have gone through so young.

Speaking to my son-in-law recently he paid great tribute to the Ghurkha regiment that fought so courageously alongside the British fighting forces and has done so for many campaigns in the past going back to times before the First World War.

John Hector

Our thanks to George Stovell for kindly loaning the following photographs:

M.V. Georgic, *ship to Malaysia*

George with his unit in Malaya.
(George 2nd row from front, 3rd left.)

After 1945

Britain has long been seen as a nation that will step in to help another country maintain peace. Some of these countries do not come under the United Nations, as now, where we are trying to maintain peace in Iraq. By helping to remove a brutal dictatorship the country now has a militant wing of insurgents dividing the country by acts of terror. I hope and pray that common sense will prevail and we can soon look forward to seeing the return of our fighting forces.

M.V. Empire Pride.
One ship out, the other, thankfully, brought them home.

Pensions

The old age pension that was relevant up to 1945 was limited to ten shillings a week, which was a reward for paying stamps while in full time employment. Many companies decided to introduce their own pension for employment related to the amount of wages that they paid to the employee for the week or month's work.

In my company I was charged two shillings and sixpence per week from my salary of three pounds ten shillings and as my wages increased annually, my pension advanced on a sliding scale relative to a pension at retirement time. Many companies estimated the age limit was sixty-five years of age and of course that meant in some cases, you could be working for a firm for fifty years, say from the age of fifteen to sixty-five, which would then give you a large retirement pension, which would be paid weekly after you left the company.

In the event of leaving the employment with the pension forecast less than the fifty years, the amount was informed to you before you left so that you knew what you were entitled to under the insurance that would have been taken out by the company with a reputable pensions' insurer. In my case I retired eight years earlier than the recognised term of employment, having already worked for thirty-nine years with the same company. The Chairman increased my salary by a large sum during the last year of my employment so that I would qualify for the higher pension. Over the last twenty-one years the pension has been regulated by a five per cent increase that the Government acknowledges to be how much the cost of living has risen.

As the years go on it seems established that the population is living longer and pensions are now having to be paid for a greater period than initially estimated. The level of three score years and ten for a man or woman's life span no longer applies and many are now living well beyond this. With this fact, the worry for the Government is how to maintain a good cost of living increase which has always been attached to the payable old age pension. At present, the work force in their thirties, forties and fifties are being encouraged by the Government to address the issue and take out private pension schemes. This will enable people in that age bracket a guaranteed, reasonable living standard which would not be subsidised by the Government but paid for out of the individual's own pension scheme. This of course has many problems as we read daily of various insurance and pension scheme operators finding it difficult to provide the amount involved for the future years now that the population is living much longer.

The problem now for the under-thirties is the amount of money they need to contribute to a pension fund that would give them a reasonable standard of living for thirty to forty years in the future. It's a well-known fact that they will not be earning sufficient money in their early, formative years to provide a large amount for a weekly pension which they would naturally feel was part of the Government's provision to make for them and not their own individual payments from their small wages. The young population is experiencing a high living standard at present such as foreign holidays, new cars, fine clothes, expensive entertainment and meals out but, the plastic card will not go on forever supporting the extended, overdue bank balances incurred at the current rate and surely must come to an end in the not too distant future.

There is a great deal of talk at Westminster to extend the usual age of sixty-five to sixty-eight years before the payment of old age pension, but as yet it is not the law and some firms are reluctant to employ beyond retirement age.

Since the high-profile Robert Maxwell theft of millions of pounds from workers' pension funds, other companies who had also borrowed funds have been forced into liquidation from their particular branch of industry. It has been found that the funds for the pensions have 'vanished into thin air'; no legal trials or prosecutions have followed.

What the Government over the last twenty years has failed to prevent is the draining of the country's income – robbing the purse of the taxes that have been paid and diverting these large sums to education, the Health Service and providing large amounts of Legal Aid to illegal immigrants whom under European and Humanitarian Group laws must be well provided for.

To take out private pensions may seem, to many people, a good idea worth considering, but from personal experience I would urge caution.

I paid, for thirty-seven years, into the company's personal pension fund, which started off at two shillings and sixpence (twelve pence) per week, and rose to £3.50 per week. This was to provide me with a lower pension income as I retired eight years below the sixty-five years qualifier. For the last thirty years, ten per cent of my monthly pension pay has been deducted, under the qualification that I am 'earning'. I am not being rewarded for the years I paid in.

Can you expect the future population of pensioners to trust in the Government to look after them, to hold on to the large sum of money needed to provide for them?

What a very poor outlook is envisaged, not for my grand-children, perhaps, for they have learned to make provisions, but I fear it will be my great grand children that will need a tremendous amount of support and guidance on how to live and survive in these costly times.

The Coronations

This book would not be complete if I failed to mention the historic years that came to an end in 1952, of a sixteen-year service to this country of a young Royal couple, the Duke and Duchess of York, who came to bear the responsibilities of the throne of England as King George VI and Queen Elizabeth upon the abdication of the then King Edward VIII; who, upon the death of King George V his father, decided to forego his reign as King in order to marry the woman he loved, an American divorcee, Mrs Wallis Simpson.

Cameos of King Edward VIII, King George VI and Queen Elizabeth, the Queen Mother

Our new King George VI and Queen Elizabeth saw in their sixteen years of service the most dramatic times this country has ever recorded. They came to the throne at the time that Germany, under the leadership of Adolf Hitler, was marching through Europe annexing countries to submit to German rule. We, at that time, had a very, very weak Conservative Government under the auspices of Neville Chamberlain, who was hell bent in keeping the peace despite the many countries suffering under the dictatorship of Germany. The crowning moment of Chamberlain's 'glory' upon his return from a meeting with Adolf Hitler in Munich, Germany, was when his plane landed at Croydon Airport and he was photographed on the steps of the aircraft waving a piece of paper that had been signed by both Adolf Hitler and Neville Chamberlain declaring "Peace in our Time". History has shown that this was a worthless treaty as Hitler had no intention of keeping the peace in any shape or form.

Our new young King and Queen with their two daughters had to bear the brunt of all the problems arising after War was declared in 1939, such a short while after accession to the throne. They witnessed Europe being torn apart, countries being invaded and defiance of all the treaties ratified after the First World War; there was no faith in the new Europe as it was progressing.

It is a fact to ponder that if King Edward VIII had continued his reign, what the outcome would have been for Britain. Edward, the then Prince of Wales, was known to have close contacts with Germany – would a peaceful armistice have ensued?

However, our new King George VI and Queen Elizabeth stood by us during those difficult days and became a couple so loved by everyone in the country. They, too, bore the brunt of the bombing and tragedies that were occurring in the United Kingdom by the assault from the German Air force on our towns and cities and the annihilation of the British expeditionary force evacuating from Dunkirk in 1940; indeed the King and Queen were nearly killed after a daylight bombing raid hit Buckingham Palace in September of that year and they lost the Duke of Kent in an air accident in

1942. The Queen was to remark that although it had been terrible to have suffered from a bombing raid at Buckingham Palace, it made her "feel able to look the East End in the face". Such terrible years for their reign.

Two weeks after the declaration of the end of the War the King and Queen visited the bomb-damaged area in the East End of London around the site of the Cotton Street Pub in East India Dock Road. This very spot was where I had narrowly missed being a victim of the massive V2 rocket that had struck the area; where I was due to have my lunch with some colleagues. Fate had a hand that day in my bus arriving fifteen minutes late after an already late departure from my office.

The heir presumptive to the English throne was, of course, Princess Elizabeth, the King and Queen's eldest daughter. At the start of 1945 she persuaded her father to allow her to undertake her National Service and she joined the ATS (the Auxiliary Transport Service) proving to be a very good driver and knowledgeable mechanic.

Coronation Cameo

John Hector

In 1952, long after the end of the War overseen by our then Prime Minister, Mr Winston Churchill, King George died in his sleep at Sandringham. His health had never been robust, with his tendency to over work, a passion for detail in all things and the added strain of the War Years, and a bout of arteriosclerosis in 1947 had left him very weak. He opened the Festival of Britain in 1951 and in the February of 1952, after another serious illness, he passed away. News of her father's death reached Princess Elizabeth and her husband, the Duke of Edinburgh, whilst they were visiting Kenya.

In the June of 1953 we had a new Queen, Elizabeth II, who with the same courage and determination as her father and mother, has given this country one of the finest reigns of over fifty years of a monarch that we are all so proud of.

It was very fitting that Mr Winston Churchill was in office as Prime Minister at the time Princess Elizabeth was crowned Queen. A man that had assured that this Great Country, Britain, would never be under the tyranny of the dictator Hitler.

Queen Elizabeth II

Epilogue

Now that the memories of post-War Britain and the make do and mend period of my life has been fully explained in the foregoing chapters, I would like my readers to appreciate the efforts that are being made to put this book into large print for those who are partially sighted like myself and whose eyes have started to fail with Macular degeneration. It is with great pleasure that I read and hear of so many advances that are now being made into the medical technology to recover and improve sight; I am most grateful for this.

As for technology itself, I have come through nearly ninety years of advancement in wonders that we never thought would arise. Space travel, television, computers that have enriched our lives, mobile telephones enabling us to have conversations across the world aided by satellite and the Internet technology of the World Wide Web are just some of the scientific developments that have radically changed our world.

I regard myself as fortunate in life to have lived longer than the remaining members of my family and in doing so and having missed death by inches on three occasions I am most grateful to be able to say that I have lived a very happy life. I have always tried to help those less fortunate and support as many charities as I am able to and I do sincerely hope that you enjoy what I have written. When these words are put on the bookshelf, long after I have left

John Hector

this planet, I hope they will be enjoyed for many years to come and I do God Bless all the readers of these few lines.

John Hector
2007

Acknowledgements

Thanks and gratitude to:

Deal Library Kent County Council

Tower Hamlets Bancroft Library (Local History Archives)

Corus Teesside Cast Products

Teesside Archives and Friends of Teesside Archives, Middlesbrough Council

Royal London Hospital Archives and Museum for photo of the London Hospital in the 1950s

Ladbrokes Middlesex

William Hill Wood Green

Best of British Magazine

Newham Archives and Local Studies, Stratford Library

Newham Recorder

Clacton Library

Darlington Railway Centre and Museum

H M Postmaster General

Imperial War Museum for photos of Monseigneur News Theatre, London, WVS running British Restaurant, Preparation of Meal, Woolmore Street Restaurant

John Hector

Leeds Central Library

Leeds City Council Learning and Leisure department library and information service for the photograph of the Leeds City News Theatre

Clacton History Society

London Metropolitan Archive Library for photos of the Festival Hall and Festival Gardens

Marguerite Patten

Philip Cone – photos of the Colchester, 1971 and the Dart American and the Dart Europa

J W Armstrong Trust

George T. Stovell – photos and cartoon sketch

www.eastlondonpostcard.co.uk for photos of Tower Bridge and the Pool of London, Port of London, Royal Docks and Millwall Dock; photos of Poplar Hospital, St Andrew's Hospital, East London Hospital for Children, City of London Hospital, Her Majesty's Hospital, Stepney Causeway

My heartfelt thanks to my lovely daughter Christine for all the care, love and help she is giving to me and of course the hundreds of hours she has spent in compiling this, my documentary, of the events that rapidly followed peacetime in 1945; these events affected millions in the years that followed and in some cases upset the future of so many thousands of people who were expecting brighter days.

My grateful thanks, also, to my fine grandson Kevin for the assistance he has given in preparing my manuscript.